**Suggested Rules of
Procedure for the Board of
County Commissioners**

Fourth Edition

Trey Allen

**Electronic
download
available**

🏛 | UNC
SCHOOL OF
GOVERNMENT

Access an Electronic Version of the Procedural Rules

Purchase of this book includes a FREE electronic version of the
procedural rules that can be customized to fit a particular board's
specific needs.

Visit the URL below to access and download the rules in RTF format:

sog.unc.edu/pubs/9781560119043

For information about other publications and resources from the
School of Government, visit sog.unc.edu.

Suggested Rules of Procedure for the Board of County Commissioners

Fourth Edition

Trey Allen

The School of Government at the University of North Carolina at Chapel Hill works to improve the lives of North Carolinians by engaging in practical scholarship that helps public officials and citizens understand and improve state and local government. Established in 1931 as the Institute of Government, the School provides educational, advisory, and research services for state and local governments. The School of Government is also home to a nationally ranked Master of Public Administration program, the North Carolina Judicial College, and specialized centers focused on community and economic development, information technology, and environmental finance.

As the largest university-based local government training, advisory, and research organization in the United States, the School of Government offers up to 200 courses, webinars, and specialized conferences for more than 12,000 public officials each year. In addition, faculty members annually publish approximately 50 books, manuals, reports, articles, bulletins, and other print and online content related to state and local government. The School also produces the *Daily Bulletin Online* each day the General Assembly is in session, reporting on activities for members of the legislature and others who need to follow the course of legislation.

Operating support for the School of Government's programs and activities comes from many sources, including state appropriations, local government membership dues, private contributions, publication sales, course fees, and service contracts.

Visit sog.unc.edu or call 919.966.5381 for more information on the School's courses, publications, programs, and services.

Michael R. Smith, Dean
Thomas H. Thornburg, Senior Associate Dean
Frayda S. Bluestein, Associate Dean for Faculty Development
Johnny Burleson, Associate Dean for Development
Michael Vollmer, Associate Dean for Administration
Linda H. Weiner, Associate Dean for Operations
Janet Holston, Director of Strategy and Innovation

FACULTY

Whitney Afonso
Trey Allen
Gregory S. Allison
David N. Ammons
Ann M. Anderson
Maureen Berner
Mark F. Botts
Anita R. Brown-Graham
Peg Carlson
Leisha DeHart-Davis
Shea Riggsbee Denning
Sara DePasquale
James C. Drennan
Richard D. Ducker
Norma Houston

Cheryl Daniels Howell
Jeffrey A. Hughes
Willow S. Jacobson
Robert P. Joyce
Diane M. Juffras
Dona G. Lewandowski
Adam Lovelady
James M. Markham
Christopher B. McLaughlin
Kara A. Millonzi
Jill D. Moore
Jonathan Q. Morgan
Ricardo S. Morse
C. Tyler Mulligan
Kimberly L. Nelson

David W. Owens
LaToya B. Powell
William C. Rivenbark
Dale J. Roenigk
John Rubin
Jessica Smith
Meredith Smith
Carl W. Stenberg III
John B. Stephens
Charles Szypszak
Shannon H. Tufts
Aimee N. Wall
Jeffrey B. Welty
Richard B. Whisnant

Printed in the United States of America

21 20 19 18 17   1 2 3 4 5

ISBN 978-1-56011-904-3

♾ This publication is printed on permanent, acid-free paper in compliance with the North Carolina General Statutes.

♻ Printed on recycled paper

About the Series

Local Government Board Builders offers local elected leaders practical advice on how to effectively lead and govern. Each of the booklets in this series provides a topic overview, and many offer specific tips on effective practice, worksheets, and reflection questions to help local elected leaders improve their work. The series focuses on common activities for local governing boards, such as selecting and appointing committees and advisory boards, planning for the future, making better decisions, improving board accountability, and effectively engaging stakeholders in public decisions.

Vaughn Mamlin Upshaw, formerly lecturer in public administration and government at the UNC School of Government, is founding editor of the series.

Other Books in This Series

Leading Your Governing Board: A Guide for Mayors and County Board Chairs, Vaughn Mamlin Upshaw, 2009

A Model Code of Ethics for North Carolina Local Elected Officials, A. Fleming Bell, II, 2010

Creating and Maintaining Effective Local Government Citizen Advisory Committees, Vaughn Mamlin Upshaw, 2010

Working with Nonprofit Organizations, Margaret Henderson, Lydian Altman, Suzanne Julian, Gordon P. Whitaker, and Eileen R. Youens, 2010

Public Outreach and Participation, John B. Stephens, Ricardo S. Morse, and Kelley T. O'Brien, 2011

Local Government Revenue Sources in North Carolina, Kara A. Millonzi, 2011

Getting the Right Fit: The Governing Board's Role in Hiring a Manager, Vaughn Mamlin Upshaw, John A. Rible IV, and Carl W. Stenberg, 2011

The Property Tax in North Carolina, Christopher B. McLaughlin, 2012

Local Government Budgeting: A Guide for North Carolina Elected Officials,
Julie M. Brenman with Gregory S. Allison, 2013

Handbook for North Carolina Mayors and Council Members, David M. Lawrence, 2013

How Are We Doing? Evaluating Manager and Board Performance,
Vaughn Mamlin Upshaw, 2014

Wicked Problems: What Can Local Governments Do? Eric M. Reese and
Maureen M. Berner, 2014

Strategic Planning for Elected Officials: Setting Priorities, Lydian Altman,
Margaret Henderson, and Vaughn Mamlin Upshaw, 2017

Suggested Rules of Procedure for a City Council, Trey Allen, Fourth Edition, 2017

Suggested Rules of Procedure for Small Local Government Boards, A. Fleming Bell, II,
Second Edition, 1998

Contents

Preface

This fourth edition of *Suggested Rules of Procedure for the Board of County Commissioners* builds on the work of Bonnie E. Davis, who authored the first edition published in 1978, and Joseph S. Ferrell, who revised and expanded the work in 1990 and again in 2002. As originally conceived, the book was an adaptation of *Robert's Rules of Order* to suit the needs of county governing boards. With its focus on large assemblies, *Robert's* is not always the ideal parliamentary authority for small bodies. The length of *Robert's*—the current edition exceeds 700 pages—and the number and complexity of its rules create significant potential for confusion. The small size of boards of county commissioners and the lack of trained parliamentarians at many of their meetings make a shorter and less complicated set of model rules desirable. Moreover, the procedural rules followed by boards of county commissioners must take into account statutory requirements that go beyond or deviate from *Robert's*.

Prior editions of *Suggested Rules of Procedure for the Board of County Commissioners* succeeded admirably in furnishing county governing boards with sample rules, manageable both in number and complexity, that satisfied both generally accepted parliamentary principles and the procedural requirements of state law. The commentary included in those editions raised issues involving the application of the rules and directed the reader's attention to pertinent statutes. Boards throughout the state recognized the value of prior editions by modeling their own procedural rules on them.

This fourth edition differs from prior editions in important ways. Intervening statutory changes have been taken into account. Rules have been reordered and categorized expressly by topic. Extensive modifications have been made to the text of rules, and explanatory comments have been added or expanded. New rules have been added, and some rules from prior editions have been eliminated, combined with other rules, or divided into separate rules.

Two primary goals underlay the revisions. The first was to make the rules easier to understand and apply whenever possible. The comment to the rule on ordinance adoption, for example, now includes a detailed explanation of how the rule's provisions work in practice. The second goal was to address recurring procedural issues not covered by prior editions. So, for instance, this edition contains rules and commentary on remote participation by members in board meetings (Rule 3) and the ability of members to change their votes (Rule 28).

Suggested Rules of Procedure for the Board of County Commissioners is a companion to the School of Government's *Suggested Rules of Procedure for a City Council,* the most recent edition of which came out earlier in 2017. In revising and updating these two books, I have endeavored to bring them into agreement except where state law or long-standing practice dictated otherwise.

Thanks are due to two of my colleagues at the School of Government. Norma R. Houston has been part of this edition from the outset. The volume's overall organization and specific approaches to many procedural issues owe much to her influence. Both Norma and Frayda S. Bluestein carefully reviewed the manuscript of this edition and provided many valuable suggestions. The fourth edition is much better than it would have been without their input. Of course, I alone bear responsibility for any remaining errors.

Trey Allen
Assistant Professor of Public Law and Government
Chapel Hill
Summer 2017

Introduction

The members of the board of county commissioners decide important issues of public policy. This reality can lead to difficult meetings, particularly when agenda items attract public scrutiny. The model rules in this volume are intended to help the board reach informed decisions in an effective, efficient, orderly, courteous, and fair manner, regardless of the matter under consideration.[1] The content of these rules reflects the influence of parliamentary law, statutory procedural requirements, *Robert's Rules of Order Newly Revised* and similar manuals, and the advising that faculty members at the School of Government have done on procedural issues over the years.

Parliamentary law encompasses the "recognized rules, precedents[,] and usages of legislative bodies by which their procedure is regulated. It is that system of rules and precedents that originated in the British Parliament and . . . has been developed by legislative or deliberative bodies in this and other countries."[2] Parliamentary law has yielded a number of fundamental principles for the conduct of business by deliberative bodies.[3] With the board of county commissioners in mind, some of the principles may be stated as follows:

- *The board must take only those actions that lie within its authority.* In North Carolina, counties have only those powers conferred on them by the General Assembly.[4]

---

1. *See* American Institute of Parliamentarians Standard Code of Parliamentary Procedure (hereinafter Standard Code) 2 (2012) ("The purpose of meeting procedures is to allow members to reach informed business decisions in an effective, efficient, orderly, courteous, and fair manner.").

2. American Society of Legislative Clerks and Secretaries' Mason's Manual Revision Commission, Mason's Manual of Legislative Procedure (hereinafter Mason's Manual) § 35, at 29 (2010 ed.).

3. The fundamental principles listed in this introduction are taken primarily from pages 1–4 of Mason's Manual and pages 6–10 of Standard Code.

4. Craig v. Cnty. of Chatham, 356 N.C. 40, 44 (2002) (noting that counties "are instrumentalities of state government and possess only those powers the General Assembly has conferred on them").

- *The board must meet in order to act.* The powers granted to the board belong to the board as a whole, not to individual members, who may not act for the board except pursuant to valid delegations of authority.
- *Members of the board are equal participants.* Each member has the right to propose motions, to debate, to vote, and to exercise any other privilege of membership. At the same time, each member is bound by reciprocal obligations, such as the duty to protect the rights of fellow members.
- *Members must receive proper notice of board meetings.* Because each member has the right to participate in meetings, members should have reasonable notice of each meeting's time, place, and purpose. This principle has been codified in statutory provisions that require member notification when the board holds a meeting that is not on its regular meeting schedule.[5]
- *A quorum is necessary for the board to act.* State law specifies the method for determining whether a quorum of the board is present.[6]
- *There must be an opportunity for debate.* The board is a deliberative body, that is, a body of persons who meet "to discuss and determine upon common action."[7] Members cannot be expected to form collective judgments unless they can exchange information and opinions concerning issues before the board.
- *Questions must be decided by voting.* Voting is the mechanism by which the board expresses its collective will.[8]
- *A majority vote is required to take action.* Inasmuch as the board operates democratically, the will of the majority is regarded as the will of the board.[9] The term "majority vote" usually means more than half of lawful votes cast, a quorum being present; however, state law or the board's own procedures may demand larger majorities for certain actions.
- *Meetings of the board must be characterized by fairness and good faith.* Part of conducting a meeting fairly is applying the board's procedural rules consistently. The consistent application of the rules ensures that members are

---

5. Section 153A-40(b) of the North Carolina General Statutes (hereinafter G.S.).

6. G.S. 153A-43. The provisions of this statute are incorporated into Rule 2 and discussed in the *Comment* thereto.

7. *Robert's Rules of Order Newly Revised* (hereinafter RONR (11th ed.)), xxix.

8. *See* STANDARD CODE 147 ("[A] vote is a formal expression of the will of the assembly.").

9. *Id.* at 135 ("[I]n an organization, the ultimate authority lies in a majority of the members when they meet to take action through majority votes. This fundamental principle of voting allows members to democratically and legitimately operate their organization.").

treated the same, whatever their viewpoints on particular issues. A member who tries to manipulate the board through fraud, trickery, or deception violates his or her obligation to act in good faith.

The above principles permeate these rules. For example, consistent with the right of members to engage in debate, Rule 32 (Motion 9) does not permit the board to entertain a motion to end debate on a pending matter until every member has had a chance to speak at least once. The requirement in Rule 27 that motions pass by majority vote recognizes the fundamental place of majority rule in deliberative bodies.

A number of these rules restate procedural requirements imposed on the board by state law. As a public body, the board must abide by the public access, notice, and other provisions of the open meetings law.[10] The demands of the open meetings law are reflected most conspicuously in Part III (Open Meetings) and Part V (Types of Meetings) of this volume. Rule 34 comports with G.S. 153A-45, the statute governing the number of votes necessary to adopt an ordinance or take any action having the effect of an ordinance. The other points at which these rules incorporate statutory requirements are too numerous to mention here but are documented in the commentary and footnotes.

Local acts can be another major source of procedural requirements. Before adopting these rules, the board should take care to determine whether one or more rules must be modified to comply with any local act by which it is bound.

Many of the specifics in these rules are not dictated by fundamental parliamentary principles or by statute. Instead, they correspond more or less to procedures recommended by *Robert's* or other prominent manuals of procedure. The board has broad discretion to modify or omit any provision that does not embody parliamentary or state law, even if the variation departs from *Robert's*.[11] For instance, the restrictions in Rule 32 on motions to reconsider—who may make them and when they may be offered—could be relaxed without violating parliamentary or state law. Similarly, although Rule 23 eliminates the practice of requiring seconds to motions, the board could substitute its own rule to the contrary.

This fourth edition of *Suggested Rules of Procedure for the Board of County Commissioners* also bears the imprint of countless hours that faculty members at the School of Government have spent advising local governments on procedural matters. Insights gained from that experience have influenced nearly everything about these rules, including decisions

---

10. G.S. 143-318.9, -318.18.

11. *See* G.S. 153A-41 ("The board of commissioners may adopt its own rules of procedure, in keeping with the size and nature of the board and in the spirit of generally accepted principles of parliamentary procedure.").

as to their organization, scope, and wording. These insights have likewise inspired features intended to improve this volume's usefulness. The commentary has been significantly expanded to address issues related to the application of these rules. Footnotes cite relevant legal and persuasive authorities. The chart in Appendix A makes it easier to navigate among procedural motions. Appendix B lists selected North Carolina General Statutes that impose procedural requirements on the board.

True to the School's mission of promoting good government, this volume has been prepared throughout with the aim of producing a piece of practical scholarship that will aid board members in performing their important duties. With that aspiration in mind, it is fitting to close with a practical recommendation. In adopting these rules, the board should not act by ordinance. Larger majorities are sometimes necessary to adopt or amend ordinances than to take other actions (compare Rule 34 with Rule 27). If it puts its procedural rules into an ordinance, the board will not be able to change them unless it can satisfy the vote requirements for ordinances.

Suggested Rules of Procedure

Part I. Applicability

Rule 1. Applicability of Rules

These rules apply to all meetings of the Board of Commissioners of _____ County. For purposes of these rules, a meeting of the board occurs whenever a majority of the board's members gather, whether in person or simultaneously by electronic means, to conduct hearings, deliberate, vote, or otherwise transact public business within the board's real or apparent jurisdiction. The term "majority" as used here and elsewhere in these rules means, unless otherwise specified, a simple majority, that is, more than half.

> **Comment:** The board of county commissioners may adopt rules of procedure, so long as they do not conflict with state law and are "in keeping with the size and nature of the board and in the spirit of generally accepted principles of parliamentary procedure."[1] The suggested rules in this volume incorporate pertinent statutory requirements, important judicial decisions on procedural issues, and general parliamentary principles. The board may need to modify one or more of these suggested rules to conform to the provisions of any local acts that apply to it.
>
> The effect of Rule 1 is to make these rules applicable to any gathering of board members covered by the open meetings law, which imposes public notice, access, and other requirements on the official meetings of public bodies.[2] For purposes of that law and these rules, members are deemed to hold an official meeting

---

1. G.S. 153A-41.
2. G.S. 143-318.9, -318.18.

whenever a majority of them come together in one place or gather simultaneously by electronic means to conduct public business within the board's real or apparent jurisdiction.[3] On the other hand, purely social and other informal gatherings do not qualify as meetings of the board, unless they are called or held to evade the spirit and purposes of the open meetings law.[4]

As indicated by the word "deliberate" in Rule 1, these rules extend to gatherings at which a majority of board members discuss county business, even if no action is taken.

Part II. Quorum

Rule 2. Quorum

The presence of a quorum is necessary for the board to conduct business. A quorum consists of a majority of the board's membership. Vacancies do not reduce the number of members necessary to establish a quorum. A member who withdraws from a meeting of the board without being excused by majority vote of the remaining members present is deemed present for quorum purposes. The board may compel an absent member to attend by ordering the sheriff to take the member into custody.

> **Comment:** This rule largely restates G.S. 153A-43. In accordance with Rule 1, the term "majority" as used here should be understood to mean a simple majority, that is, more than half.[5]
>
> General. The term "quorum" refers to the minimum number of members who must be present for a body to conduct business.[6] It usually does not refer to the number of members who vote on a particular motion.[7]
>
> The mere existence of a quorum does not always mean that the board has enough members present to take a particular action. As set out in Rule 27 and the *Comment* thereto, a simple majority—more than half—of votes cast, a quorum being present, is sufficient to adopt most motions; however, some actions that may be taken by the board are subject to larger voting requirements imposed by statute or these rules.

---

3. G.S. 143-318.10(d).
4. *Id.*
5. *See RONR* (11th ed.) 400, ll. 7–8 (noting that "[t]he word *majority* means 'more than half'").
6. *RONR* (11th ed.) 345, ll. 3–7.
7. *Id.*

See, for example, the voting requirements in Rule 34 for the adoption of ordinances on the date of introduction.

Withdrawal from meeting. By stipulating that a member who withdraws from a meeting without being excused still counts as present, G.S. 153A-43 and this rule deny any single member the power to deprive the board of a quorum merely by stepping out of the meeting room.

Quorum calculations. Perhaps the best way to understand the method for calculating a quorum of the board is through examples. Suppose the board has seven seats. Four is a majority of seven, so four members would be needed to establish a quorum. Next suppose that two members of the board have resigned, leaving the board with two vacancies. Because vacancies do not affect the quorum requirement, four members are still needed for a quorum.

Compelling attendance. Unlike other local government boards, the board of county commissioners may order the sheriff to take an absent member into custody in order to compel the member to attend a meeting. An interesting question is whether the board may issue such an order when it lacks a quorum. The placement of the compelled-attendance provision in the quorum statute seems to show that the General Assembly's intent was to provide members with an effective method of obtaining a quorum.[8] It stands to reason, then, that the absence of a quorum will not prevent the board from voting to compel the attendance of an absent member.

Remote participation. Some boards of county commissioners allow members who are not physically present to take part in meetings electronically. Rule 3 and its *Comment* address the implications of this practice for quorum calculations.

Part III. Open Meetings[9]

Rule 3. Remote Participation in Board Meetings

No member who is not physically present for a board meeting may participate in the meeting by electronic means except in accordance with a policy adopted by the board.

---

8. Under *Robert's*, one of the few things a deliberative body may do in the absence of a quorum is take measures to obtain a quorum. *RONR* (11th ed.) 347, ll. 30–32. It also may recess the meeting to another time or place or adjourn the meeting. *Id.*

9. The requirements of the open meetings law are examined in great detail in Frayda S. Bluestein & David M. Lawrence, Open Meetings and Local Governments in North Carolina: Some Questions and Answers (8th ed. 2017).

[Although a member who attends a meeting electronically pursuant to such a policy may take part in debate, the member may neither be counted toward a quorum nor vote on any matter before the board.]

> **Comment:** Although the open meetings law acknowledges the possibility of remote (electronic) participation by the members of public bodies,[10] no statute expressly authorizes members of the board of county commissioners who are not physically present to take part in the board's meetings. Consequently, if the board opts to allow remote participation, it should spell out the conditions under which members may participate in meetings via conference call, Skype, or similar devices or applications.
>
> Given the lack of explicit statutory authority for remote participation, the board runs the risk of having its actions invalidated if it relies on a member who is not in the meeting room to establish a quorum or to cast the deciding vote on a matter. The board will want to adopt the language in brackets if it prefers to avoid that risk.[11]

Rule 4. Meetings to Be Open to the Public

Except as permitted by Rule 5, all meetings of the board shall be open to the public, and any person may attend its meetings.

> **Comment:** The presumption under the open meetings law is that a public body's meetings will be open to the public.[12] The law allows a public body to enter closed session, however, for the reasons set out in G.S. 143-318.11 and Rule 5.

Rule 5. Closed Sessions

(a) Motion to Enter Closed Session. The board may enter a closed session from which the public is excluded only upon a motion duly made and adopted in open session. The motion to enter closed session must cite one or more of the permissible bases for closed session listed in paragraph (b) of this rule. A motion to enter closed session under subparagraph (b)(1) or (b)(2) must contain the additional information specified in those provisions.

---

10. G.S. 143-318.13(a).

11. For more information and analysis about the legal issues raised by remote participation by members of public bodies, see Frayda S. Bluestein, *Remote Participation in Local Government Board Meetings*, Loc. Gov't L. Bull. 133 (Aug. 2013), www.sog.unc.edu/sites/www.sog.unc.edu/files/reports/lglb133.pdf.

12. G.S. 143-318.10(a).

(b) Bases for Closed Session. A closed session is permissible under the following circumstances and no others:

(1) To prevent the disclosure of information that is privileged or confidential under the law of North Carolina or of the United States or that does not constitute a public record within the meaning of Chapter 132 of the General Statutes. The motion to enter closed session must name or cite the law that renders the information confidential or privileged.

Comment: Subparagraph (b)(1) restates G.S. 143-318.11(a)(1). Chapter 132 of the General Statutes comprises the state's public records law.

This exception applies not only to records that must be withheld from public inspection because they are confidential, but also to non-confidential records that fall outside the public records law's definition of "public records." For example, under G.S. 132-1.7(a), the term "public records" does not cover security plans or detailed plans or drawings of public buildings and infrastructure facilities. The board may enter closed session to review such plans or drawings, even though they are not confidential, and, thus, their disclosure would not violate the law.

(2) To consult with the county attorney or another attorney employed or retained by the county in order to preserve the attorney–client privilege. If the board expects to discuss a pending lawsuit with its attorney, the motion to enter closed session must name the parties to the lawsuit.

Comment: Subparagraph (b)(2) restates G.S. 143-318.11(a)(2). The open meetings law expressly prohibits a public body from discussing general policy matters when it goes into closed session to consult with its attorney. Additionally, the mere presence of the county attorney at a board meeting is not grounds for a closed session. Unless the board is going into closed session for the purpose of consulting with its attorney on a specific legal issue, it should not invoke the attorney–client privilege as a basis for closed session.

The board may enter closed session under subparagraph (b)(2) to consider and give instructions to the attorney regarding any claims, litigation, and other legal proceedings brought by or against the board. If the board considers or approves a settlement in closed session, then (unless the settlement resolves malpractice claims against a public hospital) the settlement's terms must be reported to the board in open session and entered into the board's minutes as soon as possible within a reasonable time after the settlement is reached.

The handling or settlement of claims or legal proceedings is not the exclusive basis for going into closed session to preserve the attorney–client privilege. The board may enter closed session to discuss any legal issue with its attorney. This exception may be used only if the attorney is present for the closed session, either physically or by electronic means.

(3) To discuss matters relating to (a) the location or expansion of industries or other businesses in the area served by the county or (b) the closure or realignment of a military installation. The board may reach agreement in closed session on a tentative list of economic development incentives to be offered in negotiations, but the approval of the signing of any economic development contract or commitment and the authorization of the payment of economic development expenditures must take place in open session.

Comment: Subparagraph (b)(3) restates G.S. 143-318.11(a)(4).

(4) To establish or instruct staff or agents concerning the county's position in negotiating the price or other material terms of an agreement to acquire real property by purchase, exchange, or lease.

Comment: Subparagraph (b)(4) restates part of G.S. 143-318.11(a)(5). If requested to do so, the board must disclose the following information before going into closed session: (a) the current owner of the property, (b) the property's location, and (c) the use to which the board intends to put the property.[13]

Neither G.S. 143-318.11(a)(5) nor this rule permits a closed session to discuss the sale of county property, whether real or personal. Similarly, neither provision authorizes a closed session to discuss the purchase or lease of personal property.

(5) To establish or instruct staff or agents concerning the amount of compensation or other material terms of an employment contract.

Comment: Subparagraph (b)(5) restates part of G.S. 143-318.11(a)(5).

(6) To consider the qualifications, competence, performance, character, fitness or conditions of appointment or employment of a public officer or employee or prospective public officer or employee, except when the individual in question is a member of the board or other public body or is being considered to fill a seat on the board or other public body. Final action to appoint or employ a public officer or employee must take place in open session.

Comment: Subparagraph (b)(6) restates part of G.S. 143-318.11(a)(6). The board may not go into closed session on this basis to consider general personnel policy

---

13. Boney Publishers, Inc. v. Burlington City Council, 151 N.C. App. 651, 657 (2002).

issues. It likewise in most circumstances may not enter closed session to discuss a member or prospective member of the board or any of the board's appointed bodies.

(7) To hear or investigate a charge or complaint by or against a public officer or employee. Final action discharging an employee or removing an officer must occur in open session.

Comment: Subparagraph (b)(7) restates part of G.S. 143-318.11(a)(6). This basis for closed session is largely self-explanatory, except insofar as grievances against individual board members or members of appointed bodies are concerned. It might allow the board to go into closed session to hear such a grievance, but because a board member's or an appointed board member's competence, performance, character, and fitness may not be considered in closed session, any discussion of the substance of the grievance and any action taken against the member in response to the grievance would probably have to take place in open session.

(8) To plan, conduct, or hear reports concerning investigations of alleged criminal misconduct.

Comment: Subparagraph (b)(8) restates G.S. 143-318.11(a)(7).

(9) To view a law enforcement recording released pursuant to G.S. 132-1.4A.

Comment: General Statute 132-1.4A sharply restricts the circumstances in which a law enforcement agency may disclose (make available for listening or viewing) or release (provide a copy) audio and visual recordings captured by body-worn cameras, dashboard cameras, or other recording devices operated by or on behalf of the agency or its law enforcement personnel in the performance of their duties.[14] The open meetings law allows a public body to which such a recording has been released to review it in closed session.[15]

(10) On any other basis permitted by law.

Comment: Over the years, the General Assembly has added to the list of grounds on which a public body may meet in closed session. Subparagraph (b)(10) spares the board from having to amend Rule 5 if future legislation further expands the list.

---

14. *See* Frayda Bluestein, *Answers to Questions About North Carolina's Body-Worn Camera Law*, COATES' CANONS: NC LOC. GOV'T L. BLOG (July 20, 2016), http://canons.sog.unc.edu/answers-questions-north-carolinas-body-worn-camera-law (discussing impact of laws governing access to audio and visual recordings captured by law enforcement agencies' body-worn cameras and dashboard cameras).

15. G.S. 143-318.11(a)(10).

(c) Closed Session Participants. Unless the board directs otherwise, the county manager, county attorney, and clerk to the board may attend closed sessions of the board. No other person may attend a closed session unless invited by majority vote of the board.

> **Comment:** The open meetings law does not specifically address who may attend a closed session. The board will usually want its manager, attorney, and clerk to be there, but the board may in its discretion exclude them, except that the attorney must be included when the closed session is being held to preserve the attorney–client privilege. All other non-members should be excluded from closed session, except when their presence is reasonably necessary to aid the board's deliberations. Note that in certain situations closed session attendance must be restricted due to the confidential nature of the matters under consideration. When, for instance, the board meets in closed session to consult with its attorney, the board risks waiving the attorney–client privilege if it allows someone to attend who is not covered by the privilege. Likewise, if the board enters closed session to examine county personnel records that are confidential under G.S. 153A-98, it must exclude anyone who is not authorized to access those records.

(d) Motion to Return to Open Session. Upon completing its closed session business, the board shall end the closed session by adopting a duly made motion to return to open session.

> **Comment:** The open meetings law does not list adjournment among the actions that a public body may take in closed session. Accordingly, the board must return to open session following the conclusion of a closed session, even if adjournment is the only remaining item of business.

Rule 6. Meeting Minutes

(a) Minutes Required for All Meetings. The board must keep full and accurate minutes of all of its meetings, including closed sessions. To be "full and accurate," minutes must record all actions taken by the board. They should set out the precise wording of each motion and make it possible to determine the number of votes cast for and against each motion. The minutes need not record discussions of board members, though the board in its discretion may decide to incorporate such details into the minutes.

> **Comment:** Both G.S. 153A-42 and the open meetings law mandate that full and accurate minutes be kept for all board meetings.[16] According to the North Carolina

---

16. G.S. 143-318.10(e). More precisely, G.S. 153A-42 directs the clerk to keep full and accurate minutes of the board's proceedings.

Supreme Court, minutes "should contain mainly a record of what was *done* at the meeting, not what was *said* by the members."[17] Why? Because the purpose of minutes "is to reflect matters such as motions made, the movant, points of order, and appeals—not to show discussion or absence of action."[18] Nonetheless, because the minutes belong to the board, the board may choose to record the substance of its discussions in the minutes, and many boards of county commissioners do just that.

The minutes should make clear the total number of votes cast for and against each motion. Some actions must be approved by more than a simple majority. If the board's adoption of a motion to take such an action were challenged on the ground that not enough members voted in favor of it, the court would examine the minutes to ascertain whether the requisite supermajority supported the motion.

Under the open meetings law, a public body's minutes "may be in written form or, at the option of the public body, may be in the form of sound or video and sound recordings."[19] Various statutory provisions in Chapter 153A, though, assume that written minutes are required for board meetings.[20] Moreover, because the board's minutes qualify as essential government records, guidance promulgated by the Department of Natural and Cultural Resources pursuant to G.S. 132-8.2 directs the board, within the limitations of funds available for the purpose, to create preservation duplicates of its minutes in the form of paper or microfilm copies.[21]

(b) Record of "Ayes" and "Noes." At the request of any member, the minutes shall list each member by name and record how each member voted on a particular matter.

> **Comment:** Although the minutes should indicate the number of votes cast for and against every motion, ordinarily they need not state how each member voted by name. Pursuant to G.S. 153A-42, however, the minutes must record how each member voted on a motion if any member requests that they include the "ayes" and "noes."

---

17. Maready v. City of Winston-Salem, 342 N.C. 708, 733 (1996) (internal quotation marks omitted) (emphases in original).

18. *Id.*

19. G.S. 143-318.10(e).

20. *See, e.g.,* G.S. 153A-48 (directing the clerk to the board to maintain the ordinance book "separate from the minute book of the board of commissioners").

21. Government Records Section, North Carolina Department of Natural and Cultural Resources, *Public Records Requiring Human-Readable Preservation Duplicates,* www.archives.ncdcr.gov/Portals/3/PDF/gov_lists/Human_Readable_Records_Policy.pdf?ver=2016-03-11-084032-487.

(c) General Accounts of Closed Sessions. In addition to minutes, the board must keep a general account of each closed session. The general account must be sufficiently detailed to provide a person not in attendance with a reasonable understanding of what transpired. The board may combine the minutes and general account of a closed session into one document, so long as the document contains both a complete record of actions taken and the level of detail required for a general account.

> **Comment:** According to the open meetings law, "when a public body meets in closed session, it shall keep a general account of the closed session so that a person not in attendance would have a reasonable understanding of what transpired."[22] This wording plainly requires more than a mere record of actions taken. Concerns about whether the general account of a closed session is sufficiently thorough should be referred to the county attorney.
>
> As paragraph (c) recognizes, it is common for the board of county commissioners to incorporate the minutes and general account of a closed session into a single record. There is no legal problem with that practice, so long as the record includes any actions taken by the board in closed session and enough information about what was discussed to satisfy the statutory standard for a general account.

(d) Sealing Closed Session Records. Minutes and general accounts of closed sessions shall be sealed until unsealed by order of the board or, if the board delegates the authority to unseal to one or more staff members, in accordance with guidelines adopted by the board. The sealed minutes and general account of any closed session may be withheld from public inspection, so long as public inspection would frustrate the purpose(s) of the closed session.

> **Comment:** Although the open meetings law allows a public body to withhold the minutes and general account of a closed session from public inspection for as long as necessary to avoid frustrating the purpose of the closed session,[23] the state's public records law presumes that documents made or received in the transaction of public business must be made available for inspection and copying. The board therefore should not assume that closed session records are automatically sealed without action on its part.[24] By adopting paragraph (d), the board decides that all of its closed session records will be sealed initially and remain so until they are unsealed by the board or by staff members to whom the board has delegated the

---

22. G.S. 143-318.10(e).

23. *Id.*

24. *See* David M. Lawrence, Public Records Law for North Carolina Local Governments 350 (2d ed. 2009).

authority to make such determinations pursuant to certain guidelines. Staff persons who might be entrusted with the responsibility of reviewing and unsealing closed session records include the county attorney, the county manager, the clerk to the board, or some combination thereof.

The board's guidance to staff members on unsealing closed session records should probably direct them to review those records at regular intervals and unseal them as appropriate, even when no request to inspect or copy the records is pending.[25] Such periodic reviews can reduce the likelihood that closed session records will impermissibly remain under seal beyond the point at which their release would no longer frustrate the purpose(s) for which the board entered closed session.

Rule 7. Broadcasting and Recording Meetings

(a) Right to Broadcast and Record. Any person may photograph, film, tape-record, or otherwise reproduce any part of a board meeting that must take place in open session. Except as provided in paragraph (c) of this rule, any radio or television station may broadcast any such part of a board meeting.

> **Comment:** Paragraph (a) restates G.S. 143-318.14(a).

(b) Advance Notice. Any radio or television station that plans to broadcast any portion of a board meeting shall so notify the [clerk to the board/county manager] no later than [twenty-four hours] before the meeting. The failure to provide notice is not, by itself, grounds for preventing the broadcast of a board meeting.

> **Comment:** Paragraph (b) assumes that, if provided with advance notice of a broadcast media organization's intent to cover a board meeting, county staff will be better able to accommodate the organization and minimize any interference with the meeting. The last sentence in paragraph (b) acknowledges that neither the board nor its staff has any statutory authority to exclude broadcast media for failing to give the prescribed notice.

(c) Equipment Placement. The county manager may regulate the placement and use of camera or recording equipment in order to prevent undue interference with a board meeting, so long as he or she allows the equipment to be placed where it can carry out its intended function. If the county manager determines in good faith that the equipment and personnel necessary to broadcast, photograph, or record the meeting cannot be accommodated without undue interference to the meeting, and an adequate alternative

---

25. *Id.*

meeting room is not readily available, the county manager may require the pooling of the equipment and the personnel operating it.

> **Comment:** The open meetings law vests the powers set out in paragraph (c) in the board.[26] Paragraph (c) delegates these powers to the county manager, primarily because, unlike the board, the county manager may act outside of and in advance of a meeting.
>
> The open meetings law specifies that a public body may not classify the ordinary use of camera or recording equipment as an undue interference with its meeting.[27]

(d) Alternative Meeting Site. If the news media request an alternative meeting site to accommodate news coverage, and the board grants the request, the news media making the request shall pay the costs incurred by the county in securing an alternative meeting site.

> **Comment:** Paragraph (d) is taken from G.S. 143-318.14(b).

Part IV. Organization of the Board

Rule 8. Organizational Meeting; Selection of Chair and Vice Chair

(a) Requirement to Hold Organizational Meeting. The board shall hold an organizational meeting each December to take the actions set out in this rule.

(b) Scheduling Organizational Meeting

(1) *Even-numbered years.* The board shall hold an organizational meeting at its regular meeting place at [10:00 a.m.] on the first Monday in December of each even-numbered year. [The organizational meeting shall be convened and concluded before the regular December meeting is convened.]

(2) *Odd-numbered years.* The board shall hold an organizational meeting during its first regular meeting in December.

> **Comment:** The scheduling requirements in paragraph (b) of this rule reflect the provisions of G.S. 153A-39. The statute and this rule treat even-numbered and odd-numbered years differently because the membership of the board often changes in even-numbered years due to the occurrence of county elections. The bracketed sentence in subparagraph (b)(1) should be adopted if the board would prefer that,

---

26. *See* G.S. 143-318.14(b).
27. *Id.*

following an election for one or more of its seats, any consideration of substantive matters at the December regular meeting be delayed until any newly elected members have assumed their offices.

(c) Order of Business

(1) *Even-numbered years*

(A) As the first order of business at the organizational meeting, all persons elected or reelected to the board at the most recent county election must take and subscribe the oath of office set out in Article VI, Section 7, of the North Carolina Constitution, unless they did so earlier in the day. They must then take the General Oath prescribed by G.S. 11-11. Each member's constitutional oath must be filed with the clerk to the board. Although a newly elected or reelected member who has not yet been sworn and who is not present for the organizational meeting may be sworn in later, the member must take, subscribe, and file the constitutional oath and take the G.S. 11-11 oath before he or she begins performing any of the duties of the member's office.

Comment: Article VI, Section 7, of the North Carolina Constitution expressly requires all public officers to take and subscribe the oath of office prescribed therein before they take up the duties of their offices. (An official subscribes the oath by signing beneath it.) General Statute 153A-26 echoes this requirement by directing all persons elected to county office in a general election to take and subscribe the oath of office at the board's regular meeting place on the first Monday in December, the same day that G.S. 153A-39 designates for the organizational meeting. By not expressly stating that the oath must be administered at the organizational meeting, G.S. 153A-26 leaves individuals elected to county office with the option of taking and subscribing the oath earlier (or later) in the day.

General Statute 11-7 sets out an oath of office that all state and local elected and appointed officials must take and subscribe before they enter into or take up the duties of their offices. This rule does not refer to G.S. 11-7 because the oath in that statute is substantially similar to the oath in Article VI, Section 7, and decisions from the North Carolina Supreme Court and the North Carolina Court of Appeals strongly imply that taking either oath is equivalent to taking the other.[28]

---

28. The cases referred to are *Baxter v. Nicholson*, 363 N.C. 829 (2010), and *State v. Sullivan*, 201 N.C. App. 540 (2009), which are discussed in Trey Allen, *One Oath or Two? What is THE Oath of Office?* Coates' Canons: NC Loc. Gov't L. Blog (Jan. 27, 2017), http://canons.sog.unc.edu/one-oath-or-two-what-is-the-oath-of-office.

General Statute 11-11 prescribes additional oaths for certain county officials (sheriffs, registers of deeds, county attorneys, and law enforcement officers). The statute also has a general oath for county officers not covered by its position-specific provisions, a category that includes members of the board of county commissioners. There is no subscription requirement in G.S. 11-11, so an individual does not have to sign any oath taken under this statute.

Only certain officials may administer the oath of office.[29] They include, among others, the chair, the clerk to the board, and a notary public. The deputy clerk may administer the oath in place of the clerk, if the deputy is also a sworn officer.[30]

General Statute 153A-26 expressly allows any person elected to the board who is absent during the administration of the oath of office to take and subscribe the oath later. Ordinarily the incumbent member will retain his or her seat on the board until that happens.[31]

It is imperative that incoming board members refrain from undertaking their duties before they are sworn in. Under G.S. 14-229, an individual who undertakes the duties of a public office without first taking, subscribing, and filing the oath of office is guilty of a Class 1 misdemeanor. Similarly, G.S. 128-5 provides that any person who enters upon the duties of a public office without first taking the oath of office shall be subject to a forfeiture of $500 (to be used for the poor of the county). Both statutes authorize an offender's ejectment from office. Pursuant to G.S. 153A-26, oaths of office for county officers must be filed with the clerk to the board.

(B) As the second order of business, the board shall elect a chair and vice chair from among its members using the procedure specified in Rule 39.

Comment: According to G.S. 153A-39, the board must choose a chair at the organizational meeting, unless a local act designates some other mechanism for selecting the chair. In a county where the chair is not selected by the board, neither this rule nor Rule 9 should be adopted without appropriate modifications.

Rule 39 describes the procedure the board must follow when filling a vacancy among its own members or making appointments to other public bodies. This rule directs the board to apply the same procedure to the selection of the chair and vice chair.

---

29. G.S. 11-7.1.
30. G.S. 11-8.
31. G.S. 128-7.

(C) As the third order of business, the board shall approve the bonds of [the sheriff and the register of deeds] [the sheriff, the register of deeds, and the coroner] and induct any other newly elected county officials into office.

Comment: State law requires the board to approve the sheriff's official bond on the same day as the organizational meeting.[32] It subjects the coroner's bond to the approval requirements for the sheriff's bond.[33] State law also mandates that the board approve the official bond for the register of deeds, though it is silent as to when approval must take place.[34]

This rule includes optional language that omits any reference to the coroner because the office of coroner has been abolished in many counties.

[(D) As the fourth order of business, the board may appoint the clerk to the board and the county attorney.]

Comment: Both the clerk to the board and the county attorney serve at the board's pleasure.[35] ("[A]t the board's pleasure" means that the board may vote to replace either or both of them at any regular meeting or any special meeting called for that purpose.) Given its ability to replace the clerk and the county attorney at will, the board should omit this provision if it concludes that there is no need to vote on their appointments at each organizational meeting.

(2) *Odd-Numbered Years.* As the first order of business, the board will elect the chair and vice chair. [As the second order of business, the board will vote on the appointment of the clerk to the board and the county attorney.]

Comment: No provision is made here for oath-taking or receiving the bonds of the sheriff and other county elected officials because county elections almost always occur in even-numbered years. The board should omit the bracketed sentence unless it wishes to vote on the appointments of the clerk and the county attorney at regular intervals.

(d) Presiding Officer. The outgoing chair shall call the organizational meeting to order and preside until the board elects a new chair. If the organizational meeting takes place during an even-numbered year in which the outgoing chair has lost his or her seat on the board,

---

32. G.S. 162-9.
33. G.S. 152-4.
34. G.S. 161-4.
35. G.S. 153A-111 (clerk to the board); G.S. 153A-114 (county attorney).

the [clerk to the board] shall fill the role of presiding officer until a new chair is elected. Once elected, the new chair shall preside.

> **Comment:** Local customs vary concerning who presides at the organizational meeting. In many counties the clerk to the board or the county manager presides, while in others the incumbent chair presides until the new chair is elected.
>
> Because G.S. 153A-39 designates the chair as the board's presiding officer, this rule favors having the outgoing chair preside over the organizational meeting until the board has chosen a successor. If the outgoing chair has just lost a bid for reelection to the board, however, the swearing in of the winner at the beginning of the organizational meeting or earlier in the day will immediately deprive the outgoing chair of his or her seat on the board and, thus, of the ability to preside over the board's proceedings. With that prospect in mind, paragraph (d) of this rule provides that the clerk to the board will open and preside over the organizational meeting until the board picks a new chair if the organizational meeting follows a failed reelection bid by the outgoing chair.

Rule 9. Terms of the Chair and Vice Chair

The member selected as chair at the organizational meeting shall serve for the ensuing year unless removed by the board for cause. The vice chair shall serve at the board's pleasure.

> **Comment:** According to G.S. 153A-39, the board at its organizational meeting must pick one of its members to serve as chair "for the ensuing year." By declaring that the board may remove the chair for cause, this rule assumes that the General Assembly did not intend to deprive the board of the power to remove and replace the chair for misconduct or neglect of duty.[36]
>
> Except perhaps in the most extreme cases, the board should not remove the chair before the end of his or her term without first providing the chair with notice of the alleged grounds for removal and the opportunity for a hearing. The chair may not preside over the hearing or the vote on whether to remove him or her from office. Ordinarily the vice chair, who "act[s] in the absence or disability of the chairman," should preside in such circumstances.[37] The removal of a member from the position of chair does not deprive the member of his or her seat on the board.

---

36. Under *Robert's*, an officer who serves for a fixed term may be removed from office for cause, "that is, neglect of duty or misconduct." *RONR* (11th ed.), p. 654, ll. 9–10. *See also* STANDARD CODE 185 ("An organization has an inherent right to remove an officer . . . from that position for valid cause.").

37. G.S. 153A-39.

The law does not specify the vice chair's term. Although G.S. 153A-39 might be read to imply a one-year term for the vice chair, this rule takes the position that, in the absence of clear legislative guidance to the contrary, the board may remove the vice chair at any time, with or without cause.

Part V. Types of Meetings

Rule 10. Regular Meetings

(a) Regular Meeting Schedule. The board shall hold a regular meeting on the [first and third] [Monday] of each month, except that if a regular meeting day is on a holiday on which county offices are closed, the meeting shall be held on the next business day. The meeting shall be held at [_____] and begin at [_____]. The board shall adopt a resolution establishing the meeting schedule each year consistent with this rule. For purposes of these rules, a work session of the board constitutes a regular meeting if it appears on the board's duly adopted schedule of regular meetings. In all other cases, a work session is a special meeting to which the provisions of Rule 11 apply.

> **Comment:** Pursuant to G.S. 153A-40, the board must adopt a resolution fixing the time and place for its regular meetings. If the board fails to adopt such a resolution, the statute requires it to meet at the county courthouse on the first Monday of each month or on the next business day if the first Monday is a holiday. The board must hold at least one regular meeting each month.[38]
>
> Many boards of county commissioners hold "work sessions," meetings at which members review items that may be presented for approval at "regular" meetings later in the same month. The open meetings law does not recognize work sessions as such. If a work session appears on the board's regular meeting schedule, it is a regular meeting insofar as the law is concerned. If a work session is not part of the regular meeting schedule, the board should assume that the work session triggers the law's notice requirements for special meetings.

(b) Notice of Regular Meeting Schedule. The board must ensure that a copy of its current regular meeting schedule is filed with the clerk to the board and posted on the county's website. At least 10 days before the first regular meeting held pursuant to the schedule,

---

38. According to G.S. 153A-52.1, the board must provide at least one public comment period per month at a regular meeting. It follows that the board must hold at least one regular meeting each month.

the board must cause the schedule to be published as required by law and posted [on the courthouse bulletin board].

> **Comment:** The first sentence in paragraph (b) captures the open meetings law's notice requirements for regular meetings.[39] Although the law does not require a public body without a website to post its regular meeting schedule online, paragraph (b) assumes that the county has a website. The other notice requirements in paragraph (b) come from G.S. 153A-40(a). The board does not have to post the regular meeting schedule on the courthouse bulletin board if it has adopted an ordinance designating a more appropriate or convenient location.[40]

(c) Change to Regular Meeting Schedule. The board may adopt a resolution altering the time or place of a particular regular meeting or all regular meetings within a specified period. The board must ensure that the resolution is filed with the clerk to the board at least seven (7) calendar days before the first meeting held pursuant to the revised schedule. The board must also have the revised schedule posted on the county's website. Additionally, the board must cause notice of the temporary change to be posted at or near its regular meeting place and to be sent to everyone who has submitted a written request for notice of its special meetings.

> **Comment:** The seven-day filing requirement is imposed by the open meetings law.[41] The open meetings law does not mandate posting the revised regular meeting schedule online if the county does not have a website, but this rule assumes that the county has one. The remaining notice requirements in paragraph (c) comport with G.S. 153A-40(a).

Rule 11. Special Meetings

(a) Calling Special Meetings. The chair or a majority of members may call a special meeting of the board by signing a written notice stating the date, time, and place of the meeting and the subjects to be considered.

> **Comment:** Both the open meetings law and G.S. 153A-40(b) mandate notice of special meetings.[42] The notice required by the open meetings law must state the meeting's time, location, and purpose(s).[43] Similarly, the notice provided in accor-

---

39. G.S. 143-318.12(a) & (d).
40. G.S. 153A-443.
41. G.S. 143-318.12(a).
42. G.S. 143-318.12(b).
43. G.S. 143-318.12(b)(2).

dance with G.S. 153A-40(b) must set out the meeting's time and place, as well as the subjects to be considered. Paragraph (a) assumes that listing the subjects to be considered at a special meeting qualifies as stating the meeting's purpose(s).

Pursuant to G.S. 153A-40(b), the majority necessary to call a special meeting is a majority of members, not of the number of seats on the board. Presumably this means that any vacant seats should not be counted when the number of members sufficient to call a special meeting is calculated. Thus, for example, if the board has six seats, one of which is vacant, any three of the remaining five members may call a special meeting.

(b) Notice to the Public. At least forty-eight hours before a special meeting, the board shall cause the written notice to be (1) posted on the board's principal bulletin board or, if the board has no such bulletin board, at the door of the board's usual meeting room and (2) delivered, emailed, or mailed to each newspaper, wire service, radio station, television station, and person who has filed a written request for notice with the clerk to the board. If the board's website is maintained by one or more county employees, the board must also have the notice posted there prior to the special meeting. [Furthermore, the member or members who call a special meeting are responsible for ensuring that the notice is posted on the courthouse bulletin board at least forty-eight (48) hours before the meeting.]

> **Comment:** The first two sentences in paragraph (b) incorporate the open meetings law's public notice requirements for special meetings.[44] Unless the board has adopted an ordinance designating a more appropriate or convenient location, G.S. 153A-40(b) mandates posting the notice on the courthouse bulletin board.[45]

(c) Notice to Members. At least forty-eight hours before a special meeting, the chair or the members who called the meeting shall have the written notice of the meeting delivered to the other members of the board or left at their usual dwelling places.

> **Comment:** Paragraph (c) restates notice requirements found in G.S. 153A-40(b).

(d) Transacting Other Business. Unless all members are present or any absent member has signed a written waiver of notice, only those items of business specified in the notice to members may be taken up at a special meeting. [Even when all members are present or any absent member has signed a waiver, the board may take up an item of business not covered by the notice only if the board first determines in good faith that the item must be discussed or acted upon immediately.]

---

44. G.S. 143-318.12(b)(2), (e).
45. G.S. 153A-443.

Comment: Under G.S. 153A-40(b), a special meeting of the board may address matters not listed in the notice provided to members only if all members are in attendance or any absent member has signed a written waiver of notice. The bracketed optional sentence in paragraph (d) places a further restriction on the board's ability to turn to matters at a special meeting that were not listed on the notice to members. Specifically, the bracketed sentence declares that the board may not take up such a matter unless it first concludes in good faith that the item must be discussed or acted upon immediately. This restriction is intended to reduce the likelihood of a violation of the open meetings law, which, as noted in the *Comment* to paragraph (a), requires the public notice of a special meeting to articulate the meeting's purpose. While nothing in the open meetings law expressly prohibits the board from taking up an unannounced matter at a special meeting if the requirements of G.S. 153A-40(b) are met, the bracketed sentence in paragraph (d) assumes that the board should avoid doing so when the matter is not urgent.[46]

Rule 12. Emergency Meetings

(a) Calling Emergency Meetings. The chair or a majority of the board's members may call an emergency meeting to address generally unexpected circumstances that demand the board's immediate attention.

Comment: Under G.S. 153A-40, an emergency meeting of the board is classified as a type of special meeting. Thus, the rules for who may call a special meeting apply to the calling of an emergency meeting.

(b) Notice of Emergency Meetings. The member or members who call an emergency meeting must take reasonable action to inform the other members of the board and the public of the meeting. In addition, notice of the meeting must be given to each local newspaper, local wire service, local radio station, and local television station that has filed with the clerk to the board a written request to be notified of emergency meetings. To be valid, the request must include the newspaper's, wire service's, or station's telephone number. Notice may be given by telephone, email, or the same method used to notify board members. Notice must be provided immediately after members have been notified and at the expense of the media organization notified.

---

46. *See generally* Trey Allen, *Statutory Permission to Take Up Items Not on the Special Meeting Notice*, COATES' CANONS: NC LOC. GOV'T L. BLOG (Jan. 26, 2015), http://canons.sog.unc.edu/statutory-permission-to-take-up-items-not-on-the-special-meeting-notice (analyzing the impact of statutory notice provisions on the ability of a board of county commissioners or city council to consider at a special meeting matters not included on the special meeting notice).

Comment: The first sentence in paragraph (b) incorporates the notice requirements that G.S. 153A-40 imposes on emergency meetings of the board. The remaining notice requirements come from the open meetings law.[47]

(c) Transaction of Other Business Prohibited. Only business connected with the emergency may be discussed or otherwise considered at an emergency meeting.

Comment: Both G.S. 153A-40 and the open meetings law restrict the board's ability to take up other matters at an emergency meeting.[48] Paragraph (c) combines those restrictions.

Rule 13. Recessed Meetings

(a) Calling Recessed Meetings. When conducting a properly called regular, special, or emergency meeting, the board may recess the meeting to another date, time, or place by a procedural motion made and adopted in open session, as provided in Rule 32 (Motion 3). The motion must state the time (including the date, if the meeting will resume on a different day) and place at which the meeting will reconvene.

(b) Notice of Recessed Meetings. If the board's website is maintained by one or more county employees, notice of the recessed meeting's date, time, and place must appear on the webpage prior to the meeting. No further notice of a properly called recessed meeting is required.

Comment: This rule follows the open meetings law's requirements for recessed meetings.[49] The procedural mechanism for setting a recessed meeting is a motion to recess to a time and place certain (Rule 32, Motion 3). The motion must be made in open session, since the open meetings law does not identify the adoption of such a motion as an action that may be taken during closed session.[50]

Rule 14. Limited Authority to Meet Outside the County

The board must hold all of its meetings within the county except for the following:

- a joint meeting of the board with another public body, if the joint meeting is held within the political subdivision represented by the other public body;

---

47. G.S. 143-318.12(b)(3).

48. *Id.* ("Only business connected with the emergency may be considered at a meeting to which notice is given pursuant to this paragraph."); G.S. 153A-40(b) ("Only business connected with the emergency may be discussed at a meeting called pursuant to this paragraph.").

49. G.S. 143-318.12(b)(1), (e).

50. *See* G.S. 143-318.11 (listing the grounds on which a public body may enter closed session).

- a retreat, forum, or similar gathering held solely to provide board members with general information relating to the performance of their duties, so long as members do not vote or otherwise transact business during the event;
- a meeting between the board and the local legislative delegation during a session of the General Assembly, provided board members do not vote or otherwise transact public business during the meeting except with regard to matters pertaining directly to legislation proposed to or pending before the General Assembly; and
- a convention, association meeting, or similar gathering but only if board members confine their deliberations to event-related issues that are not legally binding on the board or its constituents, such as convention resolutions and the elections of association officers.

> **Comment:** This rule restates the limitations imposed by G.S. 153A-40(c) on out-of-county meetings of the board.

Part VI. Agenda

Rule 15. Agenda

(a) Draft Agenda

(1) *Preparation.* The [clerk to the board] shall prepare a draft agenda in advance of each meeting of the board. For a regular meeting, a request to have an item of business placed on the draft agenda must be received by the [clerk] at least [two] working days before the date of the meeting. The [clerk] must place an item on the draft agenda in response to a board member's timely request.

(2) *Supplemental information/materials.* The agenda packet shall include the draft agenda, any proposed ordinances or amendments to ordinances, and supporting documentation and background information relevant to items on the agenda.

(3) *Delivery to board members.* Except in the case of an emergency meeting, each member shall receive a paper or electronic copy of the draft agenda and agenda packet at least [twenty-four hours] before the meeting.

(4) *Public inspection.* The draft agenda and agenda packet will be available to the public when they are ready to be circulated.

Comment: No statute requires the board to use an agenda. Because of the volume and complexity of the matters they confront, most boards of county commissioners use agendas for most or all of their meetings anyway.

This rule describes a typical agenda preparation process. In some counties, the county manager or the board chair may take the lead in drafting the agenda. The board in such a county may wish to modify the language to subparagraph (a)(1) to reflect that practice.

Boards of county commissioners use agendas for any or all of three reasons.

- To organize the materials that the board plans to consider. If the board makes use of agendas primarily for this reason, it is usually willing to allow last-minute additions to the agenda, if the add-ons are supported by a majority of members present and voting. That is the approach followed by this rule.

- To control the length of their meetings. When this is the main reason for having an agenda, the board will often hold an advance work session so that members may ask questions and thoroughly explore proposals to be acted upon at their regular "business" meeting. In such cases, the board may not wish to allow any late additions to the agenda unless an unexpected and pressing matter arises.

- To enable members to study matters prior to the meetings at which they will be considered. With this rationale in mind, subparagraph (a)(4) requires that members have access to the agenda packet in advance of non-emergency meetings.

There is some uncertainty in the law over the point at which a draft agenda and the rest of the agenda packet must be made available for inspection or copying in response to a public records request. The case law in North Carolina does not provide a clear answer to this question, but the safe approach seems to be to regard a draft agenda and agenda packet as public records as soon as they are ready for circulation.[51] Their status as public records does not mandate that the county advertise their existence or post them online, however, merely that they be made available in response to public records requests. Redaction may be necessary or permissible to the extent that the agenda packet contains confidential, privileged, or non-public records. If the board posts draft agendas and/or agenda packets online in a format that permits a person to view and print or save them, the county has

---

51. *See* LAWRENCE, *supra* note 24, at 15 ("[A] court might exclude . . . a draft [that is still in a very preliminary form] from the definition of public record, at least until the authority begins to circulate it to others, but there appears to be little other room for excluding from public access documents that are closer to completion.").

no legal obligation to provide paper copies of the posted documents in response to public records requests.[52]

(b) Adoption of the Agenda

(1) *Adoption.* As its first order of business at each meeting, the board shall review the draft agenda, make whatever revisions it deems appropriate, and adopt the agenda for the meeting.

(2) *Amending the agenda.* Both before and after it adopts the agenda, the board may add or subtract agenda items by majority vote of the members present and voting, except that

- the board may not add to the items stated in the notice of a special meeting unless the requirements in Rule 11(d) are satisfied and
- only business connected with the emergency may be discussed or otherwise considered at an emergency meeting.

(3) *Designation of items "For Discussion and Possible Action."* The board may designate an agenda item "for discussion and possible action." The designation signifies that the board intends to discuss the item and may, if it so chooses, take action on the item following the discussion.

Comment: Although the board enjoys broad discretion in deciding what business it will conduct at a regular meeting, procedural requirements imposed by state law on certain undertakings prevent the board from taking some actions without warning. For instance, the board may not amend the text of a zoning ordinance, even at a regular meeting, unless the published notice and public hearing mandated by G.S. 153A-323 have been provided.[53]

As explained in the *Comment* to Rule 11(d), the board runs some risk of violating the open meetings law if, at a special meeting, it takes up matters that did not appear in the public notice of the meeting. Subparagraph (b)(2) of this rule therefore prohibits adding items to the agenda for a special meeting, except in compliance with Rule 11(d). Likewise, in accordance with G.S. 153A-40(b) and G.S. 143-318.12(b)(3), the agenda for an emergency meeting is confined by subparagraph (b)(2) to business connected with the emergency.

---

52. *See* S.L. 2017-10, § 2.9 (amending G.S. 132-6 and 132-6.1).

53. Notice of the public hearing on the proposed adoption, amendment, or repeal of a zoning ordinance must be published twice in a newspaper of general circulation, once a week for two successive calendar weeks, with publication of the first notice occurring not fewer than 10 days and not more than 25 days before the hearing date. G.S. 153A-323(a).

It is commonplace for board members to want to discuss an issue informally, even when they are unsure about whether they will ultimately take action on the matter. Under subparagraph (b)(3), by designating particular agenda items "for discussion and possible action," the board preserves the option of taking action if discussion leads to agreement on a course of action.

(c) Consent Agenda. The board may designate part of an agenda for a regular meeting as the *consent agenda*. Items may be placed on the consent agenda by the person(s) charged with preparing the draft agenda if they are judged to be noncontroversial and routine. Prior to the board's adoption of the meeting agenda, the request of any member to have an item moved from the consent agenda to unfinished business must be honored by the board. All items on the consent agenda must be voted on and adopted by a single motion, with the minutes reflecting the motion and vote for each item.

> **Comment:** The consent agenda groups together items that the individuals who prepare the draft agenda regard as noncontroversial and routine. This procedural tool can improve efficiency by enabling the board to dispose of multiple matters with a single motion and vote.
>
> The board reviews the consent agenda during its examination of the draft agenda at the beginning of a meeting. Each member is free to ask for the removal of one or more items from the consent agenda. Such a request must be honored, and the item(s) in question must usually be treated as unfinished business. The board may then approve the remaining items on the consent agenda simultaneously through the adoption of a single motion. As a matter of law, the board's action constitutes a motion and vote on each item, and in keeping with this understanding, the minutes should record a separate motion and vote for each item approved as part of the consent agenda.
>
> Because the consent agenda is voted on at the outset of a meeting, items likely to generate significant public interest should not be placed on the consent agenda, especially when there will be a public comment period. If the board uses the consent agenda to dispose of controversial as well as routine matters before the public comment period, members of the public may conclude that the board does not value their input.
>
> The consent agenda should not mix items with different voting requirements. If the minimum number of affirmative votes necessary for adoption is not the same for all items on the consent agenda, the board could create a situation in which some but not all of the consent agenda has been approved. A motion to approve the minutes of a prior meeting, for example, passes so long as it receives more than

half of the votes cast, a quorum being present. On the other hand, as explained in more detail in the *Comment* to Rule 34, a unanimous vote of all members is usually necessary to approve a proposed ordinance on the date of introduction.

(d) Informal Discussion of Agenda Items. The board may informally discuss an agenda item even when no motion regarding that item is pending.

> **Comment:** Standard parliamentary practice does not permit debate on a matter in the absence of a pending motion.[54] Small boards, though, can often benefit from informal discussion prior to the making of any motion. Indeed, *Robert's Rules of Order* expressly allows small boards—defined as boards with twelve or fewer members—to engage in informal discussion of an issue while no motion is pending.[55] Paragraph (d) of this rule follows *Robert's* on this point. If informal discussion results in a motion, debate on the motion should be conducted pursuant to Rule 26.

Rule 16. Acting by Reference to Agenda or Other Document

The board shall not deliberate, vote, or otherwise take action on any matter by reference to the agenda or any other document unless copies of the agenda or document are available for public inspection at the meeting and so worded that people at the meeting can understand what is being deliberated or acted upon.

> **Comment:** This rule incorporates the open meetings law's restrictions on the ability of public bodies to act by reference.[56]

Rule 17. Agenda Items from Members of the Public

If a member of the public wishes to request that the board include an item on its regular meeting agenda, he or she must submit the request to the [clerk to the board] by the deadline specified in Rule 15(a)(1). The board is not obligated to place an item on the agenda merely because such a request has been received.

> **Comment:** While it is not unusual for members of the public to ask that an item be placed on the board's meeting agenda, the board has no legal obligation to honor such requests. The open meetings law guarantees the public's right to attend board meetings, but control of the agenda belongs to the board. Yet a total refusal

---

54. *RONR* (11th ed.) 34, ll. 7–9.
55. *RONR* (11th ed.) 488, ll. 7–8.
56. G.S. 143-318.13(c).

to consider agenda requests from residents and other interested persons could lead to negative perceptions of the board. This rule creates a mechanism for the submission of agenda requests while plainly stating that the board may choose not to act on them.

Rule 18. Order of Business

Items shall be placed on a regular meeting agenda according to the order of business. The usual order of business for each regular meeting shall be as follows:

- adoption of the agenda,
- approval of the consent agenda,
- approval of the previous meeting minutes,
- public hearings,
- public comments,
- administrative reports,
- committee reports,
- unfinished business, and
- new business.

Without objection, the chair may call agenda items in any order most convenient for the dispatch of business.

> **Comment:** This rule's placement of public hearings and the public comment period ahead of reports and unfinished and new business benefits members of the public in two ways: (1) they may address the board without having to stay for the whole meeting, and (2) they have the chance to comment on items of new or unfinished business prior to action by the board. Likewise, by putting reports before old and new business, the suggested order of business may afford at least some staff and committee members the option of leaving prior to adjournment.
>
> For purposes of these rules, unfinished business consists of matters carried over from a previous meeting, either because the board adjourned without completing its order of business or because it adopted a motion postponing the matters until the present meeting.[57]

---

57. This motion would be made in accordance with Rule 32, Motion 10 (Motion to Postpone to a Certain Time).

Part VII. Role of the Presiding Officer

Rule 19. The Chair

(a) Presiding Officer. The chair shall preside at meetings of the board.

> **Comment:** Although state law invests the chair with few formal powers, it expressly designates the chair as the board's presiding officer.[58]

(b) Voting by the Chair. [The chair has the same duty to vote as other members, though in no event may the chair break a tie on a motion on which he or she has already voted.] [The chair is excused from voting except in the case of a tie vote.]

> **Comment:** Like his or her fellow members, the chair generally has a duty to vote on all questions that come before the board. Under G.S. 153A-39(2), however, the board may adopt a rule excusing the chair from voting. The board's preference in this matter will determine its choice between the alternative provisions in paragraph (b).

(c) Recognition of Members. A member must be recognized by the chair or (or other presiding officer) in order to address the board, but recognition is not necessary for an appeal pursuant to Rule 32 (Motion 1).

> **Comment:** Standard parliamentary practice does not permit a member to address a body until he or she has first been recognized by the presiding officer.[59] On the other hand, the presiding officer must recognize any member who seeks the floor and is entitled to it.[60] Additionally, under Rule 32 (Motion 1), if a member's purpose in seeking the floor is to appeal a procedural ruling by the chair, the member may make the appeal regardless of whether the chair recognizes him or her. If recognition by the chair were necessary in that situation, the chair could defeat the appeal simply by refusing to call on the member.

(d) Powers as Presiding Officer. As presiding officer, the chair is to enforce these rules and maintain order and decorum during board meetings. To that end, the chair may

---

58. G.S. 153A-39(2). *See also* Vaughn M. Upshaw, *County and City Governing Boards, in* County and Municipal Government in North Carolina 31 (Frayda S. Bluestein ed., 2d ed. 2014) (summarizing the chair's powers). Other powers granted to the chair by state law include the power to declare a state of emergency, if the board has adopted an ordinance delegating such authority to the chair, and to call special and emergency meetings. G.S. 166A-19.22(a); G.S. 153A-40(b).

59. *RONR* (11th ed.) 376, ll. 13–16.

60. *RONR* (11th ed.) 376, l. 16; 377, l. 1.

(1) rule on points of parliamentary procedure, to include ruling out of order any motion clearly offered for obstructive or dilatory purposes;

(2) determine whether a member or other speaker has gone beyond reasonable standards of courtesy in his or her remarks and entertain and rule on objections from other members on this ground;

(3) entertain and answer questions of parliamentary procedure;

(4) call a brief recess at any time; and

(5) adjourn in an emergency.

> **Comment:** The term "recess" is defined in *Robert's Rules of Order* as "a short intermission in the assembly's proceedings, commonly of only a few minutes, which does not close the meeting and after which business will immediately be resumed at exactly the point where it was interrupted."[61]
>
> Subparagraph (d)(4) of this rule allows the chair to call for a brief recess in the belief that members can sometimes benefit from a "cooling off" period, especially when contentious topics are under consideration.[62] Ideally, in his or her capacity as presiding officer, the chair will be well placed to ascertain when a short break might help ease tensions at a meeting of the board.
>
> When to adjourn is normally a decision for the board to make through a motion and vote, but subparagraph (d)(5) authorizes the chair to adjourn a board meeting "in an emergency." The equivalent provision in *Robert's* offers some guidance regarding the type of event that would justify an emergency adjournment by the chair: "In the event of a fire, riot, or other extreme emergency, if the chair believes taking time for a vote on adjourning would be dangerous to those present, he should declare the meeting adjourned. . . . "[63]

(e) Appeals of Procedural Rulings. A member may appeal a decision made or answer given by the chair under subparagraph (d)(1), (2), or (3) in accordance with Rule 32 (Motion 1).

---

61. *RONR* (11th ed.) 230, ll. 20–23.

62. The chair's unilateral authority to call for a brief recess goes beyond the powers of presiding officers under *Robert's Rules of Order*. According to *Robert's*, a recess may be taken only on a motion and vote by the members, except when a recess is provided for in the meeting agenda. *RONR* (11th ed.) § 20, at 230–33.

63. *RONR* (11th ed.) 86, ll. 26–29.

Rule 20. Presiding Officer in the Chair's Absence

The vice chair shall preside over meetings of the board in the chair's absence. If both the chair and vice chair are absent, the members present may choose a temporary chair from among themselves. The vice chair or other member presiding in place of the chair has the powers listed in Rule 19(d). Service as presiding officer does not relieve the vice chair or other member of the duty to vote on all questions except as excused from voting pursuant to Rule 29.

> **Comment:** General Statute 153A-39(2) declares that the vice chair is "to act in the absence or disability of the chairman." It further provides that, "[i]f the chairman and vice chairman are absent from a meeting of the board, the members present may choose a temporary chairman." This rules clarifies that (1) the vice chair or other member has the same powers as the chair when presiding in place of the chair and (2) filling in for the chair does not eliminate a member's duty to vote under G.S. 153A-44 and Rule 29.

Rule 21. When the Presiding Officer Is Active in Debate

If the chair becomes active in debate on a particular proposal, he or she [may] [must] have the vice chair preside during the board's consideration of the matter. If the vice chair is absent or is also actively debating the matter, the chair [may] [must] designate another member to preside until the matter is concluded. Similarly, if while presiding, the vice chair or temporary chair wishes to join in debating a topic, he or she [may] [must] designate another member to preside for the duration of the board's consideration of the matter.

> **Comment:** When it comes to presiding officers, good leadership depends, to a certain degree, on not taking sides during a debate. If the presiding officer does take a position in debate, members on the other side of an issue might suspect that any procedural rulings detrimental to their cause result more from the presiding officer's desire to promote a certain outcome than from the impartial application of parliamentary principles. Yet on a small board, especially one composed of elected officials chosen to represent the people, it may not always be feasible or even desirable for the presiding officer to withhold his or her views. By providing that the gavel may or must be temporarily relinquished, this rule makes it possible for the chair or other presiding officer to participate in a debate without unduly compromising his or her reputation for even-handedness.

Part VIII. Motions and Voting

Rule 22. Action by the Board

Except as otherwise provided in these rules, the board shall act by motion. Any member may make a motion.

> **Comment:** There are three situations in which these rules empower the board to act by procedural mechanisms other than a motion and vote. Rule 28 provides that a member's request to change his or her vote may be granted by unanimous consent in certain situations. Rule 30 permits the board to determine by unanimous consent that it will vote on a pending motion by written ballot. Finally, Rule 38 directs the board to act by nomination rather than by motion when filling vacancies on the board or appointed bodies.

Rule 23. Second Not Required

No second is required on any motion.

> **Comment:** It is standard parliamentary practice to refuse to entertain any motion that does not receive a second. The purpose of requiring a second "is to prevent time from being consumed by the assembly's having to dispose of a motion that only one person wants to see introduced."[64] This rationale makes sense as applied to large bodies. It would be grossly inefficient, for example, for a 100-member body to debate a motion that not one of its members is willing to second. This reasoning is not persuasive as to small boards, where even a single member constitutes a significant percentage of a board's total membership. On a five-member board, for instance, a motion presumably starts with the backing of 20 percent of the members. The limited utility of seconds in the case of small boards is acknowledged by *Robert's Rules of Order*, which recommends that small boards not require seconds for motions.[65]
>
> When it comes to the board of county commissioners, the representative function of members also militates against demanding a second. Arguably, because each member speaks not just for himself or herself but for the member's constituents as well, a motion warrants the board's attention, regardless of whether another member is willing to second it.

---

64. *RONR* (11th ed.) 36, ll. 28–31.
65. *RONR* (11th ed.) 488, l. 1.

Rule 24. One Motion at a Time

A member may make only one motion at a time.

> **Comment:** "The purpose of meeting procedures is to allow members to reach informed . . . decisions in an effective, efficient, orderly, courteous, and fair manner."[66] Permitting members to make more than one motion at a time would undermine that purpose by creating enormous potential for confusion.

Rule 25. Withdrawal of Motion

The member who introduces a motion may withdraw the motion unless the motion has been amended or put to a vote.

> **Comment:** Under *Robert's Rules of Order*, the member who makes a motion may withdraw it without anyone's consent until the presiding officer states the motion.[67] Once the motion has been stated by the presiding officer, ownership of the motion transfers to the body, and the member may not withdraw it without the body's consent.[68] The *Robert's* approach seems unduly restrictive for small boards, so this rule permits a member of the board who has made a motion to withdraw it unless the board has made the motion its own by amending it or the presiding officer has called for a vote on the motion.

Rule 26. Debate

The presiding officer shall state the motion and then open the floor to debate, presiding over the debate according to the principles listed below.

- The maker of the motion is entitled to speak first.
- A member who has not spoken on the issue shall be recognized before a member who has already spoken.
- To the extent practicable, debate shall alternate between proponents and opponents of the measure.
- [No member may speak more than twice on the same substantive motion. A member's first speech on a substantive motion shall be limited to [ten] minutes, and any second speech on the same motion shall be limited to [five] minutes. The same

---

66. Standard Code 2.
67. *RONR* (11th ed.) 295, ll. 31–33.
68. *RONR* (11th ed.) 296, ll. 21–25.

rules apply to debate on a procedural motion, except that a member's first speech shall not exceed [five] minutes, and any second speech shall be limited to [two] minutes.]

> **Comment:** The first three principles set out in this rule follow guidelines for debate found in *Robert's Rules of Order*.[69] The suggested language in brackets at the end of this rule is similar to Rule 10(b) in the procedural rules for the North Carolina House of Representatives. Not every board of county commissioners will find it desirable to include the suggested language, and any board that decides to adopt it should carefully evaluate whether its proposed time limits suit the board's particular situation.

Rule 27. Adoption by Majority Vote

A motion is adopted if supported by a simple majority of the votes cast, a quorum being present, except when a larger majority is required by these rules or state law.

> **Comment:** Consistent with general parliamentary practice, this rule provides that a motion passes in most instances if supported by more than half of the votes cast, so long as a quorum is present.[70] Yet some actions require more than a simple majority of votes cast. For example, as reflected in Rule 34, state law generally prohibits the board from adopting an ordinance on the same day it is introduced, unless all board members vote in favor of the ordinance.[71] Furthermore, a supermajority is needed to adopt some of the procedural motions listed in Rule 32.
>
> Not every statutory supermajority requirement is represented in these rules. The board should consult its attorney about whether a proposed action requires more than a simple majority.

Rule 28. Changing a Vote

A member may change his or her vote on a motion at any time before the presiding officer announces whether the motion has passed or failed. Once the presiding officer announces

---

69. *RONR* (11th ed.) 379, ll. 10–13, 27–35; 380, ll. 1–2.

70. "[T]he basic requirement for approval of an action or choice by a deliberative assembly, except where a rule provides otherwise, is a *majority vote*. The word *majority* means 'more than half'; and when the term *majority vote* is used without qualification . . . it means more than half of the votes cast by persons entitled to vote, excluding blanks or abstentions, at a regular or properly called meeting." *RONR* (11th ed.) 400, ll. 5–12 (emphases in original).

71. G.S. 153A-45.

the result, a member may not change his or her vote without the unanimous consent of the remaining members present. A member's request for unanimous consent to change a vote is not in order unless made immediately following the presiding officer's announcement of the result.

> **Comment:** This rule largely adopts but also simplifies the approach taken by *Robert's Rules of Order* to vote changes.[72] Members need not actually cast votes to grant a colleague's request for unanimous consent to change a vote. The presiding officer may simply ask whether there is any objection and, hearing none, pronounce the request approved.[73]

Rule 29. Duty to Vote

(a) Duty to Vote. Every board member[, other than the chair,] must vote except when excused from voting as provided by this rule.

(b) Grounds for Excusal. A member may be excused from voting on a matter involving the member's own financial interest or official conduct, though not if the proposal in question is one to alter the compensation or allowances paid to board members. Members may also be excused from voting when prohibited from voting under G.S. 14-234 (contract providing direct benefit to member), G.S. 153A-340(g) (legislative zoning decision likely to have a direct, substantial, and readily identifiable financial impact on member), or G.S. 160A-388(e)(2) (member's participation in quasi-judicial decision would violate affected person's right to an impartial decision maker). [Questions about whether a basis for excusal exists should be directed to the county attorney.]

(c) Procedure for Excusal

(1) *At the member's request.* Upon being recognized at a duly called meeting of the board, a member who wishes to be excused from voting shall so inform the presiding officer, who must then submit the matter to a vote of the remaining members present. If a majority of the remaining members present vote to excuse the member, the member is excused from voting on the matter.

(2) *On the board's initiative.* Even when a member has not asked to be excused from voting on a matter, a majority of the remaining members present may by motion

---

72. *See RONR* (11th ed.) 408, ll. 21–36; 409, ll. 1–10 (detailing the steps necessary for a vote change). *See also* Trey Allen, *When May a Board Member Change a Vote?* Coates' Canons: NC Loc. Gov't L. Blog (June 15, 2015), http://canons.sog.unc.edu/when-may-a-board-member-change-a-vote (same).

73. *RONR* (11th ed.) 54, ll. 13–29.

and vote excuse the member from voting if the member is prohibited from voting under paragraph (b).

(d) Consequence of Non-Excused Failure to Vote. If a member who has not been excused from voting fails to vote on a matter, the member's failure to vote shall be recorded as [an affirmative] [a negative] vote, provided

(1) the member is physically present in the meeting room or
(2) the member has physically withdrawn from the meeting room without being excused by majority vote of the remaining members present.

> **Comment:** General Statute 153A-44 imposes a duty to vote on each member except when the board excuses a member for one or more of the reasons set out in the statute. (As noted in the *Comment* to Rule 19, the board may adopt a rule relieving the chair of the duty to vote in most situations.) It is not always easy to determine whether a basis for excusal exists, so the bracketed sentence at the end of paragraph (b) advises the board to consult the county attorney when it is unsure about whether excusal is proper.[74] Paragraph (c) of this rule outlines procedures for excusing members from voting when appropriate grounds exist.
>
> What happens if a member refuses to vote despite not having been excused by the board? The statute is silent on this point. Under the equivalent law for city councils, a council member's unexcused failure to vote must be recorded as an affirmative vote if the member (1) is present or (2) has stepped out without first having been excused by the remaining members present.[75] This rule adopts that approach, though the bracketed options acknowledge that the board may prefer to treat a member's unexcused failure to vote as a vote in the negative rather than as one in the affirmative. What if the board prefers to record a member's non-excused failure to vote as an abstention? General Statute 153A-44 does not expressly foreclose that option. Nonetheless, the board should consider whether recording a non-excused failure to vote as an abstention undermines the duty to vote by minimizing the impact of a member's refusal to fulfill his or her statutory voting obligation.

---

74. For a helpful overview of the ethical conflicts that can justify excusal, see Frayda S. Bluestein & Norma R. Houston, *Ethics and Conflicts of Interest, in* County and Municipal Government in North Carolina 115–24 (Frayda S. Bluestein ed., 2d ed. 2014).

75. G.S. 160A-75.

Rule 30. Voting by Written Ballot

(a) Secret Ballots Prohibited. The board may not vote by secret ballot.

(b) Rules for Written Ballots. The board may decide by majority vote or unanimous consent to vote on a motion by written ballot. Each member must sign his or her ballot, and the minutes must record how each member voted by name. The ballots must be made available for public inspection in the office of the clerk to the board immediately following the meeting at which the vote took place and remain there until the minutes of that meeting are approved, at which time the ballots may be destroyed.

> **Comment:** This rule paraphrases the open meetings law's provisions on a public body's use of written ballots.[76] Although the board may decide by majority vote to cast written ballots on a motion, paragraph (b) also allows it to make such a determination by unanimous consent to avoid the awkwardness of members voting on how to vote. The steps for obtaining unanimous consent are described in the *Comment* to Rule 28.

Rule 31. Substantive Motions

A substantive motion is not in order if made while another motion is pending. Once the board disposes of a substantive motion, it may not take up a motion that presents essentially the same issue at the same meeting, unless it first adopts a motion to reconsider pursuant to Rule 32 (Motion 14).

> **Comment:** A substantive motion is one that brings new business before the board, such as a motion to adopt an amendment to a zoning ordinance.[77] A substantive motion may propose any action within the board's legal authority. Moreover, because Rule 22 requires the board to proceed by motion, a substantive motion is typically the only way the board may act.
>
> A foundational principle of parliamentary procedure is that only one substantive proposal may be considered at any one time.[78] This rule therefore prohibits the introduction of a substantive motion while another motion is pending.

---

76. G.S. 143-318.13(b).

77. *RONR* (11th ed.) 100, ll. 3–4 ("[A] *main motion* is a motion whose introduction brings business before the assembly[.]"). There is no mention in *Robert's Rules of Order* of substantive motions as such; the equivalent term in *Robert's* is main motion. *See generally RONR* (11th ed.) § 10 (describing characteristics of a main motion).

78. *See RONR* (11th ed.) 100, ll. 4–5 (noting that a main motion "can be made only when no other motion is pending").

To promote efficiency, and consistent with *Robert's*, this rule also generally prevents the board from revisiting the subject matter of a substantive motion during the same meeting at which the motion was adopted or defeated.[79] The exception is when the board adopts a motion to reconsider the substantive motion, as provided in Rule 32 (Motion 14).

Rule 32. Procedural Motions

(a) Certain Motions Allowed. The board may consider only those procedural motions listed in this rule. Unless otherwise noted, each procedural motion may be debated and amended and requires a majority of votes cast, a quorum being present, for adoption.

> **Comment:** For purposes of these rules, a procedural motion is any non-substantive motion. In most instances, a procedural motion, if adopted, acts on a substantive motion in some way, such as a motion to postpone the board's consideration of a substantive motion until its next regular meeting.
>
> The array of motions in *Robert's Rules of Order* that would qualify as procedural motions under these rules could prove bewildering. This rule retains only those procedural motions that seem likely to aid the board in its conduct of business, and many of them have been modified to make them more user-friendly.
>
> Several of the procedural motions in *Robert's* are not subject to debate, which makes sense in that *Robert's* was written primarily with large assemblies in mind.[80] Valid concerns about efficiency can justify a large assembly's decision not to afford every member the right to speak on any and all motions. These rules favor debate on all motions, however, for three reasons: (1) the board's small size makes extended debate on most procedural motions unlikely; (2) each board member should be heard in debate because members represent not only themselves but also their constituents; and (3) procedural mechanisms such as Motion 9 (below) can bring debate to a close if it becomes too time-consuming.

(b) Priority of Motions. The procedural motions set out in this paragraph are listed in order of priority. A procedural motion is not in order so long as another procedural motion of higher priority is pending, except that

- any procedural motion other than an appeal under Motion 1 is subject to amendment as provided in Motion 12, and

---

79. *See RONR* (11th ed.) 111, ll. 11–15 (observing that typically "[n]o main motion is in order that presents substantially the same question as a motion that was finally disposed of earlier in the same session").

80. Under *Robert's*, for example, a motion to suspend the rules is not debatable. *RONR* (11th ed.) 261, l. 12.

- a motion to call the question (end debate) may be made with regard to any procedural motion in accordance with Motion 9.

When several procedural motions are pending, voting must begin with the procedural motion highest in priority, except that a motion to amend or end debate on the highest priority motion must be voted on first.

> **Comment:** As in *Robert's*, here the order of priority establishes which procedural motion yields to which—that is, which procedural motions may be made and considered while another procedural motion is pending.[81]
>
> The procedural motions described in this rule are summarized in table form in Appendix A.

Motion 1. To Appeal a Ruling of the Presiding Officer. Any member may appeal the presiding officer's ruling on whether a motion is in order or on whether a speaker has violated reasonable standards of courtesy. The presiding officer's response to a question of parliamentary procedure may also be appealed by any member. An appeal is in order immediately after the disputed ruling or parliamentary response and at no other time. The member who moves to appeal need not be recognized by the presiding officer, and if timely made, the motion may not be ruled out of order.

> **Comment:** Rule 19(e) recognizes that members may appeal the presiding officer's rulings on most procedural matters and answers to questions of parliamentary procedure. Motion 1 is the vehicle for such an appeal. It is accorded the highest priority among procedural motions, in part because it is untimely if not made immediately. Another reason for ranking it first among procedural motions is to ensure that rulings on all other procedural motions are subject to appeal.

Motion 2. To Adjourn. This motion may be used to close a meeting. It is not in order if the board is in closed session.

> **Comment:** Unlike the motion to adjourn described in *Robert's*, this motion is debatable and amendable.[82] Like the *Robert's* motion to adjourn, this motion may interrupt deliberation on a pending matter.[83] Why should the board be allowed to adjourn when business is pending? Because a vote to adjourn in such

---

81. *See generally RONR* (11th ed.) 61, ll. 11–35; 62, ll. 1–10 (explaining *RONR's* basic approach to ranking motions).

82. *RONR* (11th ed.) 236, ll. 7–8.

83. *RONR* (11th ed.) 233, ll. 17–33.

circumstances would signal that the board is not prepared to take action on one or more pending matters, and these rules disfavor forcing the board to act before it is ready.

Motion 3. To Recess to a Time and Place Certain. This motion may be used to call a recessed meeting as permitted under Rule 13. The motion must state the time (including the date, if the meeting will reconvene on a different day) and place at which the meeting will resume. The motion is not in order if the board is in closed session.

Comment: This motion is analogous to the motion to fix the time for an adjourned meeting in *Robert's*, though, unlike that motion, this motion is debatable.[84] In deference to the open meetings law, which allows a public body to "recess[] a regular, special, or emergency meeting" to another "time and place," these rules employ the term "recessed meeting" instead of "adjourned meeting."[85]

Motion 4. To Take a Brief Recess.

Comment: This motion allows the board to pause a meeting for a few minutes. It should not be confused with a motion to recess to a time and place certain under Motion 3. In contrast to *Robert's*, these rules allow debate on a motion to take a brief recess.[86] If debate on the motion becomes prolonged, the chair may render both the motion and the debate superfluous by unilaterally recessing the meeting for a short time pursuant to Rule 19(d)(4).

Motion 5. To Follow the Agenda. This motion must be made at the time an item of business that deviates from the agenda is proposed; otherwise, the motion is out of order as to that item.

Comment: This motion is loosely patterned on the call for the orders of the day in *Robert's*, though unlike a call for the orders of the day, a motion to follow the agenda is debatable.[87] If adopted, it curtails the chair's freedom under Rule 18 to call agenda items out of order. If the board as a whole does not object to the deviation from the agenda, it may simply vote down the motion. Alternatively, the board may pass the motion but then amend the agenda in accordance with Rule 15(b)(2).

---

84. *See generally* RONR (11th ed.) § 22 at 242–46 (outlining the chief characteristics of a motion to fix the time to which to adjourn).

85. G.S. 143-318.12(b)(1). *See also* G.S. 153A-40(a) ("The board may adjourn a regular meeting from day to day or to a day certain until the business before the board is completed.").

86. *RONR* (11th ed.) 231, l. 30.

87. *See generally* RONR (11th ed.) 219, ll. 1–20; 220, ll. 1–35; 221, ll. 1–18 (discussing key features of the call for the orders of the day).

Motion 6. To Suspend the Rules. To be adopted, a motion to suspend the rules must receive affirmative votes equal to at least a quorum of the board. The board may not suspend provisions in these rules that are required under state law.

> **Comment:** This motion is generally the same as the motion to suspend the rules in *Robert's*, except that it is debatable and amendable.[88] This motion is in order when the board wishes to take some action within its legal authority but one or more of these rules prevents it from doing so. For example, the board could use this motion in the middle of a regular meeting to permit consideration of a proposed noise ordinance that is not on the agenda. (Of course, the board could reach the same result by amending the agenda to add the proposed noise ordinance.)
>
> The requirements of state law may limit the board's ability to suspend its rules in certain situations. For instance, the board may not suspend the rules to add to its agenda action on a proposed amendment to a zoning ordinance unless it has complied with the statutory public notice and hearing requirements that apply to such measures.[89] Some provisions in these rules incorporate requirements of state law and, therefore, may not lawfully be suspended. For example, the board may not suspend the notice requirements for special meetings set out in Rule 11 because they are compulsory under the open meetings law and G.S. 153A-40.
>
> A motion to suspend the rules fails unless it receives affirmative votes equal to at least a quorum of the board's membership. Thus, the number of votes required to suspend the rules is greater than the number required to pass most motions except when the board has no vacancies and all members are present and voting. The purpose of this elevated vote threshold is to discourage the board from departing from its rules in the ordinary course of business.

Motion 7. To Divide a Complex Motion. This motion is in order whenever a member wishes to consider and vote on parts of a complex motion separately. The member who makes this motion must specify how the complex motion will be divided.

> **Comment:** This motion can help simplify debate on a complex proposal, particularly when members' support for or opposition to the proposal's component parts

---

88. *See generally* RONR (11th ed.) § 25, at 260–67 (describing characteristics of the motion to suspend the rules).

89. *See* G.S. 153A-323 (setting out procedures for adopting, amending, and repealing zoning and other development ordinances). *See also* David Owens, *Mandated Notices in Land Development Regulations*, Coates' Canons: NC Loc. Gov't L. Blog (Jan. 28, 2014), http://canons.sog.unc.edu/mandated-notices-in-land-development-regulations (summarizing the notice requirements that apply to the adoption, amendment, and repeal of development ordinances).

is not uniform. Aside from being debatable, it is roughly equivalent to the motion for division of a question in *Robert's*.[90]

Motion 8. To Defer Consideration. The board may defer its consideration of a substantive motion, and any proposed amendments thereto, to an unspecified time. A motion that has been deferred expires unless the board votes to revive it pursuant to Motion 13 within [100] days of deferral. A new motion having the same effect as a deferred motion may not be introduced until the latter has expired.

> **Comment:** This motion is a hybrid of two motions in *Robert's*: the motion to postpone indefinitely and the motion to lay on the table.[91] If adopted, a motion to postpone indefinitely effectively kills the pending substantive motion at which it takes aim, thereby enabling a deliberative body to defeat the substantive motion without actually voting on it.[92] In contrast, a motion to lay on the table allows a deliberative body to set aside a pending substantive motion temporarily when a matter demanding immediate attention arises.[93] The body may return to the tabled motion later through the adoption of a motion to remove from the table.[94]
>
> Under these rules, the motion to defer consideration is the proper mechanism for killing a substantive motion indirectly or for delaying consideration of it temporarily. If the board's goal is to kill the substantive motion indirectly, it merely has to adopt a deferral motion and leave the substantive motion in limbo until the period during which a motion to revive consideration (Motion 13) would be in order elapses, at which time the substantive motion automatically expires. If the objective is to put off consideration of the substantive motion temporarily, the board may accomplish its goal by adopting a deferral motion and later voting within the prescribed number of days to revive consideration. Like a motion to postpone indefinitely and a motion to table, a motion to defer consideration may

---

90. *See generally RONR* (11th ed.) § 27, at 270–76 (discussing main features of the motion for division of a question).

91. *See generally RONR* (11th ed.) § 11, at 126–30 (describing characteristics of the motion to postpone indefinitely); *RONR* (11th ed.) § 17, at 209–18 (setting out the rules that apply to a motion to lay on the table).

92. *RONR* (11th ed.) 126, ll. 4–7 ("*Postpone Indefinitely* is a motion that the assembly decline to take a position on the main question. Its adoption kills the main motion . . . and avoids a direct vote on the question. It is useful in disposing of a badly chosen main motion that cannot be either adopted or expressly rejected without possibly undesirable consequences.").

93. *RONR* (11th ed.) 209, ll. 26–30 ("The motion to *Lay on the Table* enables the assembly to lay the pending question aside temporarily when something else of immediate urgency has arisen or when something else needs to be addressed before consideration of the pending question is resumed. . . .").

94. *RONR* (11th ed.) 300, ll. 3–5 ("The object of the motion to *Take from the Table* is to make pending again before the assembly a motion or a series of adhering motions that previously has been laid on the table[.]").

include both a pending substantive motion and any pending motions to amend the substantive motion.

In general, the board may not consider a new substantive motion that would have the same effect as a deferred motion until the deadline for reviving the latter has passed. Of course, if the board is determined to take up the new motion while the deferred motion remains pending, it may do so under Motion 6 by voting to suspend its rules to allow consideration of the new motion.

The motion to defer consideration should be distinguished from Motion 10, which may be used to postpone consideration of a substantive motion to a designated time. A substantive motion that has been postponed to a certain time must be brought up again at the time specified. No motion to revive is needed.

Motion 9. To End Debate (Call the Previous Question). If adopted, this motion terminates debate on a pending motion, thereby bringing it to an immediate vote. This motion is not in order until every member has had an opportunity to speak once on the pending motion.

Comment: Many people wrongly assume that a member may bring debate on a pending motion to a close simply by saying, "I call the question," or words to that effect. A body that allows a single member to end debate in that way offends the fundamental parliamentary principle of majority rule. If a majority of members want debate on a matter to continue, no single member should have the power to override their will. Furthermore, allowing a single member to decide when debate must end could infringe on the right of other members to participate equally in the debate.

Under both *Robert's* and these rules, the words "I call the question" amount to a motion to end debate on a pending matter.[95] If a member calls the question when more than one motion is pending, the presiding officer should ensure that the member specifies the motion(s) on which he or she would like debate to stop.

Motion 9 differs from the motion for the previous question in *Robert's* in three significant respects. First, it is debatable.[96] Second, whereas *Robert's* allows a member to call the question at almost any point during a debate, provided the member has been recognized, Motion 9 bars the calling of the question until every member has had a chance to speak at least once.[97] Third, *Robert's* requires a two-

---

95. *RONR* (11th ed.) 202, ll. 5-10.

96. *RONR* (11th ed.) 200, l. 1.

97. A member may not interrupt another member to move the previous question. *RONR* (11th ed.) 199, l. 30.

thirds majority to bring debate to a close, but a simple majority of votes cast is enough to end debate under these rules.[98]

Motion 10. To Postpone to a Certain Time. This motion may be employed to delay the board's consideration of a substantive motion, and any proposed amendments thereto, until a designated day, meeting, or hour. During the period of postponement, the board may not take up a new motion raising essentially the same issue without first suspending its rules pursuant to Motion 6.

> **Comment:** This motion is similar to the motion to postpone to a certain time (or definitely) in *Robert's*.[99] It allows the board to postpone consideration of a matter until a particular day, meeting, or hour. The motion is appropriate when the board needs more information or deliberations on the matter are likely to be lengthy.
>
> This motion should be distinguished from the motion to defer consideration (Motion 8), which can postpone the board's consideration of a matter indefinitely.

Motion 11. To Refer a Motion to a Committee. The board may vote to refer a substantive motion to a committee for study and recommendations. While the substantive motion is pending before the committee, the board may not take up a new motion raising essentially the same issue without first suspending its rules pursuant to Motion 6. If the committee fails to report on the motion within [60] days of the referral date, the board must take up the motion if asked to do so by the member who introduced it.

> **Comment:** The analogous motion in *Robert's* does not grant the introducer of a proposal the power to force consideration of the proposal if the committee to which it has been referred fails to act.[100] By creating such a right, these rules make it harder for other board members to defeat a proposal by sending it to a committee that will just "sit" on it. Of course, if the board does not use committees, this motion is unnecessary.

---

98. *See RONR* (11th ed.) 200, ll. 24–30; 201, ll. 1–2 (noting that *Robert's* imposes a supermajority requirement on the motion for the previous question because otherwise "a temporary majority of only one vote could deny the remaining members all opportunity to discuss any measure that such a majority wished to adopt or kill"). The rationale in *Robert's* for requiring a supermajority to end debate does not apply here because Motion 9 is not in order until every board member has had the opportunity to speak at least once on the motion in question.

99. *See generally RONR* (11th ed.) § 14, at 179–91 (setting out the rules applicable to a motion to postpone to a certain time (or definitely)).

100. Under *Robert's*, when a body wishes to take up a matter that it has previously referred to a committee, the adoption of a motion to discharge a committee is usually necessary. *RONR* (11th ed.) 310, ll. 31–33; 311, ll. 1–5.

Motion 12. To Amend.

(a) Germaneness. A motion to amend must concern the same subject matter as the motion it seeks to alter.

> **Comment:** An amendment is germane if it *"in some way involve[s]* the same question that is raised by the motion to which it is applied."[101] An amendment is not germane if it introduces a question that is unrelated to the one posed by the original motion, but "an amendment can be hostile to, or even defeat, the spirit of the original motion and still be germane."[102] Of course, if the intent is to defeat the original motion, the most efficient way to accomplish that objective is to vote against the original motion.
>
> In *Robert's* a motion to amend by deleting and replacing much or all of the original motion is referred to as a "motion to substitute" and is governed by its own subset of procedures.[103] To avoid confusion, these rules require both major and minor changes to be proposed through a motion to amend.
>
> If the member who made the original motion disapproves of a pending motion to amend, he or she is free under Rule 25 to withdraw the original motion, so long as no other proposed amendment to the motion has been adopted. If the original motion is withdrawn, another member may put the same issue to the board in the form of a new motion.

(b) Limit on Number of Motions to Amend. When a motion to amend is under consideration, a motion to amend the amendment may be made; however, no more than one motion to amend and one motion to amend the amendment may be pending at the same time.

> **Comment:** Consistent with *Robert's*, and to reduce the likelihood of confusion, these rules allow only one motion to amend (primary amendment) and one motion to amend the amendment (secondary amendment) to be pending simultaneously.[104] Such amendments are voted on in reverse order; that is, the secondary amendment is voted on first. Once the secondary amendment has been disposed of, another secondary amendment may be offered. The same is true for primary amendments.[105]

(c) Amendments to Ordinances. Any amendment to a proposed ordinance must be reduced to writing before the vote on the amendment.

---

101. *RONR* (11th ed.) 136, ll. 8–9 (emphasis in original).
102. *RONR* (11th ed.) 136, ll. 17–19.
103. *RONR* (11th ed.) 153–62.
104. *RONR* (11th ed.) 135, ll. 27–30.
105. *Id.*

Comment: When the amendment in question is to a proposed ordinance, this rule directs that the amendment be put in writing before the board votes on it. One reason for this mandate is that, if the amendment is adopted and the ordinance passes, the amended ordinance may impose legal obligations or restrictions on people, businesses, or other entities within the county. It seems prudent to reduce matters of such importance to writing prior to a vote so that board members will fully understand the change(s) they are being asked to make. Additionally, by putting all amendments to proposed ordinances in writing, the board will make it easier for its clerk to update the county's ordinance book pursuant to G.S. 153A-48 and to ensure that the amendments are incorporated into the code of ordinances, if the county has one, in accordance with G.S. 153A-49.

Motion 13. To Revive Consideration. The board may vote to revive consideration of any substantive motion that has been deferred pursuant to Motion 8, provided it does so within [100] days of its vote to defer consideration.

Comment: This motion replaces the motion to take from the table in *Robert's*.[106] It has been renamed to make its connection with Motion 8 apparent. Unlike the motion to take from the table, this motion may be debated and amended.[107] If the motion to revive consideration of a deferred motion is not adopted within the prescribed number of days, the deferred motion expires, though at that point the same issue presented by the deferred motion could be reintroduced in the form of a new substantive motion. The number of days specified in Motion 8 and Motion 13 should be the same.

Motion 14. To Reconsider. The board may vote to reconsider its action on a matter, provided the motion to reconsider is made (a) at the same meeting during which the action to be reconsidered was taken and (b) by a member who voted with the prevailing side. For purposes of this motion, "the same meeting" includes any continuation of a meeting through a motion to recess to a certain time and place (Motion 3). The motion is not in order if it interrupts the board's deliberation on a pending matter.

Comment: The restrictions on who may move to reconsider and when a motion to reconsider may be offered correspond to limitations imposed on the parallel motion in *Robert's*.[108]

---

106. *See generally* RONR (11th ed.) § 34, at 300–04 (describing characteristics of the motion to take from the table).

107. *RONR* (11th ed.) 301, ll. 22–23.

108. *RONR* (11th ed.) 315, ll. 28–31; 316, ll. 22–26.

The "prevailing side" is usually the majority, but not always. Some actions require more than a simple majority for approval. (The adoption of a proposed ordinance on the date of introduction under Rule 34 is one example.) If a motion to take such an action garners a simple majority but not the necessary supermajority, the members who voted against the motion constitute the prevailing side, even though they were in the minority.[109] If a motion fails due to a tie vote, the members who voted against the motion are the prevailing side.

The limitation on when a motion to reconsider may be made should not be understood to prevent the board from reversing itself at a subsequent meeting. In general, the board is free to undo an action taken at a prior meeting, except when reversal would violate the law by, for instance, infringing on vested rights or breaching the terms of a valid contract.

The board may reverse an action taken at a previous meeting in either of two ways. It may pass a new motion that has the opposite effect of the one previously adopted. Alternatively, as permitted by Motion 15, the board may vote to rescind or repeal the prior action.

The motion to reconsider is allowed under these rules only when action on a pending matter concludes.

Motion 15. To Rescind. The board may vote to rescind an action taken at a prior meeting provided rescission is not forbidden by law.

> **Comment:** Each meeting of the board is in many respects a separate legal event. Consequently, and as noted in the *Comment* to Motion 14, the board may at a subsequent meeting undo an action taken at a previous meeting, except when prohibited by law, as when rescission would violate vested rights or result in the breach of a valid contract.
>
> In contrast to a motion to reconsider, a motion to rescind may be made at any time, and by any member, after the meeting at which the action to be reversed was taken.

Motion 16. To Prevent Reintroduction for [Six] Months. This motion may be used to prevent the reintroduction of a failed substantive motion for a time, but it is in order only when made immediately following the substantive motion's defeat. To be adopted, this motion must receive affirmative votes equal to at least a quorum of the board. If this

---

109. In its section on motions to reconsider, *Robert's* acknowledges that, when a motion requires a supermajority for adoption, the minority can be the "prevailing side" if the motion fails. *RONR* (11th ed.) 315, ll. 34–36; 316, l. 1.

motion is adopted, the ban on reintroduction remains in effect for [six] months or until the board's next organizational meeting in an even-numbered year, whichever occurs first.

> **Comment:** This "clincher" motion can be used to prevent a member from introducing the same motion again and again when the board as a whole has no desire to consider it further. The objection to consideration of a question in *Robert's* serves a similar purpose.[110]
>
> The elevated vote requirement for this motion recognizes that members should not lightly act to curtail another member's right to bring a matter before the board. If the board later wishes to take up the matter during the period in which reintroduction is forbidden, it may do so by suspending the rule under Motion 6.
>
> Six months is merely a suggested time; the board may shorten or lengthen the time as it sees fit. In order to give new board members a clean slate, the motion is not effective beyond the board's next organizational meeting following a general election of county commissioners.

Part IX. Ordinances and Contracts

Rule 33. Introduction of Ordinances

For purposes of these rules, the "date of introduction" for a proposed ordinance is the first date on which [the proposed ordinance appears on the approved agenda for a board meeting] [the board actually considers the proposed ordinance] [the board votes on whether to adopt or make changes to the proposed ordinance].

> **Comment:** Under G.S. 153A-45, as explained more fully in Rule 34 and the *Comment* thereto, the size of the majority necessary to approve a proposed ordinance may depend on whether the vote takes place on the date of introduction. The statute does not define "date of introduction," and there are no court cases interpreting the term. In the absence of legislative and judicial guidance, county attorneys have offered various opinions about what constitutes the date of introduction. This rule gives the board three definitions to pick from, ranging from least to most restrictive. The more restrictive the approach, the more likely it is that an

---

110. *RONR* (11th ed.) 267, ll. 16–20 ("The purpose of an *Objection to the Consideration of a Question* is to enable the assembly to avoid a particular original main motion altogether when it believes it would be strongly undesirable for the motion even to come before the assembly.").

ordinance will survive a lawsuit claiming that the ordinance did not receive the requisite majority because the board misidentified the date of introduction.[111]

Rule 34. Adoption, Amendment, and Repeal of Ordinances

(a) Form of Proposed Ordinances. The board may not adopt a proposed ordinance unless it has been reduced to writing and distributed to members before the vote is taken.

(b) Adoption of Ordinances Not Subject to Public Hearing Requirements.

(1) *Approval on date of introduction.* To be adopted at the meeting where first introduced, an ordinance or any action having the effect of an ordinance must receive the affirmative votes of all members of the board. If the measure receives a majority of votes cast on the date of introduction but not the unanimous support of all members, the board must take it up again at its next regular meeting.

(2) *Approval after date of introduction.* At its first regular meeting following the date of introduction or at any meeting thereafter within 100 days of the date of introduction, the board may adopt the proposed ordinance or action having the effect of an ordinance by a majority of votes cast, a quorum being present.

Comment: Paragraph (b) of this rule largely paraphrases G.S. 153A-45. The statute's unanimity requirement does not apply to the budget ordinance or other ordinances for which the board must hold public hearings prior to adoption, such as zoning ordinances or ordinances naming or renaming county roads.[112] The remaining remarks in this *Comment* concern the many types of ordinances not subject to public hearing requirements, such as noise ordinances and public nuisance ordinances.

Note that a member's absence will prevent the board from adopting an ordinance on the date of introduction. The plain language of the statute requires the affirmative votes of all members, not just the affirmative votes of all members

---

111. The third and most restrictive option in this rule is influenced by G.S. 160A-75, the voting statute for city councils. In contrast to G.S. 153A-45, the city voting statute defines "date of introduction" as the date on which "the subject matter [of an ordinance] is first voted on by the council." It is possible that a court would read the city statute's definition into G.S. 153A-45. It is also possible that a court would regard the omission of a definition in G.S. 153A-45 as a decision by the legislature to afford boards of county commissioners with more flexibility than G.S. 160A-75 provides to city councils.

112. G.S. 153A-239.1 (procedures requirements for naming or renaming county roads); 153A-323 (procedures for adopting, amending, or repealing zoning and other development ordinances). For a list of the various statutes requiring cities to hold public hearings, see Appendix 2 in BLUESTEIN & LAWRENCE, *supra* note 9, at 111–13.

present. What if a member's death or resignation leaves the board with a vacancy? The statute does not address this issue. Accordingly, even if the board's remaining members vote unanimously in favor of a proposed ordinance on the date of introduction, the prudent course is to bring the measure back at a later meeting for a second vote. When the board votes on a proposed ordinance at a meeting subsequent to, but within 100 days of, the date of introduction, all that is necessary for adoption is a majority (more than half) of votes cast, a quorum being present.

The following scenario illustrates how the provisions of G.S. 153A-45 and paragraph (b) work in practice.

- Suppose the board has seven members and no vacancies. Four members make up a quorum of the board. For the board to adopt a proposed noise ordinance on the date of introduction, all seven members must vote for the proposal. Assume that two members are absent from the regular monthly meeting but that all five of the board's other members vote in favor of adopting the proposed ordinance. The motion fails for lack of a sufficient majority, but the board must take up the proposal at its next regular meeting because it was approved by a majority of members voting.

- Only four members show up for the board's next regular meeting. This time the proposed noise ordinance receives three affirmative votes and one negative vote. The ordinance has been adopted because it received a majority of votes cast, a quorum being present, within 100 days of the date of introduction.

If the board fails to approve a proposed ordinance within 100 days of the date of introduction, the unanimity requirement applies the next time the board takes up the matter.

(c) Adoption of Ordinances Subject to Public Hearing Requirements.

(1) *The budget ordinance or budget amendments.* Rule 35 governs the approval of the budget ordinance and amendments thereto.

(2) *Other ordinances.* Following a required public hearing on a proposed ordinance, the board may adopt the measure by a majority of votes cast, a quorum being present, regardless of whether the vote occurs on the date of introduction.

Comment: As observed in the *Comment* to Rule 35, G.S. 159-17 establishes procedures for the approval of the budget ordinance and budget amendments.

(d) Amendment and Repeal of Ordinances.
The same voting requirements that govern the adoption of proposed ordinances also apply to the amendment or repeal of an ordinance.

Comment: The voting requirements in G.S. 153A-45 pertain not only to motions to adopt ordinances but also to motions to amend or repeal ordinances. As courts in other states and influential treatises on local government law have acknowledged, a local governing board must act by ordinance to amend or repeal an ordinance.[113] Consistent with this principle, the same notice and hearing requirements that govern the adoption of zoning and other development ordinances apply to their amendment or repeal.[114]

Rule 35. Adoption of the Budget Ordinance

(a) Special Rules for the Adoption or Amendment of the Budget Ordinance. Notwithstanding any provision in general law or any local act,

(1) the board may adopt or amend the budget ordinance at a regular or special meeting of the board by a majority of those members present and voting, a quorum being present;

(2) no action taken with respect to the adoption or amendment of the budget ordinance need be published or is subject to any other procedural requirement governing the adoption of ordinances or resolutions by the board; and

(3) the adoption or amendment of the budget ordinance and the levy of taxes in the budget ordinance are not subject to the provisions of any local act concerning initiative or referendum.

(b) Notice Requirements for Budget Meetings. During the period beginning with the submission of the budget to the board and ending with the adoption of the budget ordinance, the board may hold any special meetings that may be necessary to complete its work on the budget ordinance. Except for the notice requirements of the open meetings law, which continue to apply, no provision of law or these rules concerning the call of special meetings applies during that period, so long as

---

113. *See, e.g.,* Cent. Realty Corp. v. Allison, 63 S.E.2d 153, 158 (S.C. 1951) ("Ordinarily, a municipal ordinance cannot be amended or repealed by a mere resolution. To accomplish that result a new ordinance must be passed.") (internal quotation marks omitted); 6 McQuillin Mun. Corp. § 21:13 (3d ed.) ("The general rule is that an ordinance cannot be amended, repealed or suspended by an order or resolution, or other act by a council of less dignity than the ordinance itself. Generally, an ordinance cannot be amended, repealed, or suspended by a resolution."). *See also* Trey Allen, *Repealing Ordinances,* Coates' Canons: NC Loc. Gov't Law Blog (Nov. 13, 2015), http://canons.sog.unc.edu/repealing-ordinances (analyzing the law pertaining to ordinance repeal).

114. G.S. 153A-323(a).

(1) each member of the board has actual notice of each special meeting called for the purpose of considering the budget and

(2) no business other than consideration of the budget is taken up.

(c) No Authority for Closed Sessions. This rule shall not be construed to authorize the board to hold closed sessions on any basis other than the grounds set out in Rule 5.

> **Comment:** With minor modifications, this rule restates G.S. 159-17, which creates an exception to ordinance voting requirements for the budget ordinance and budget amendments.
>
> Paragraph (b) acknowledges that the notice requirements of the open meeting law apply to meetings held to work on the budget ordinance. It eliminates, however, the need to comply with the provisions in G.S. 153A-40 and Rule 11 concerning notice to individual board members, so long as each member receives actual notice of any special meeting called to consider the budget.
>
> When more than the initial meeting is necessary to finish the budget ordinance, the board may hold one or more recessed meetings to complete its work.

Part X. Public Hearings and Comment Periods

Rule 36. Public Hearings

(a) Calling Public Hearings. In addition to holding public hearings required by law, the board may hold any public hearings it deems advisable. The board may schedule hearings or delegate that responsibility to county staff members, as appropriate, except when state law directs the board itself to call the hearing. If the board delegates scheduling authority, it must provide adequate guidance to assist staff members in exercising that authority.

> **Comment:** Some boards of county commissioners allow staff members to schedule public hearings on their behalf. Paragraph (a) sanctions that practice except when otherwise limited by law, but it also requires an explicit delegation of authority by the board and clear guidelines for the exercise of the delegated authority. Courts are often very particular about the procedural requirements for public hearings. The board should do what it can to ensure that staff members follow statutory and any board-established procedures when they schedule public hearings.

(b) Public Hearing Locations. The board may hold public hearings anywhere within the county.

> **Comment:** Paragraph (b) restates the geographic limitation on public hearings imposed by G.S. 153A-52.

(c) Notice of Public Hearings. Any public hearing at which a quorum of the board is present shall be considered part of a regular or special meeting. Consequently, the relevant notice and related requirements of the open meetings law, as set out in Rules 10 through 13, apply to such hearings. Some statutes mandate additional notice for particular types of hearings, and such notice must be provided together with the notice required by the open meetings law.

> **Comment:** A public hearing triggers the notice, minutes, and other requirements of the open meetings law if a majority of board members are present for the hearing, since under those circumstances the event qualifies as an official meeting of the board. Depending on the topic of the hearing, other statutory notice requirements may have to be satisfied as well.[115]

(d) Rules for Public Hearings. The board may adopt reasonable rules for public hearings that, among other things,

- fix the maximum time allotted to each speaker,
- provide for the designation of spokespersons for groups of persons supporting or opposing the same positions,
- provide for the selection of delegates from groups of persons supporting or opposing the same positions when the number of persons wishing to attend the hearing exceeds the capacity of the meeting room (so long as arrangements are made, in the case of a hearing subject to the open meetings law, for those excluded from the meeting room to listen to the hearing), and
- provide for the maintenance of order and decorum in the conduct of the hearing.

> **Comment:** Paragraph (d) incorporates provisions in G.S. 153A-52 regarding rules for public hearings. In keeping with the spirit of the open meetings law, it also dictates that group members desiring to be present at a hearing covered by that law be given the opportunity to listen to the proceedings—outside the meeting room if necessary—if the room is too small to accommodate them.

---

115. For a list of the various statutes requiring cities to hold public hearings, see Appendix 2 in Bluestein & Lawrence, *supra* note 9, at 111–13.

(e) Continuing Public Hearings. The board may continue any public hearing without further advertisement to a time and place certain, provided the time (including the date, if the hearing will resume on a different day) and place of the continued hearing are announced in open session. Except for hearings conducted pursuant to paragraph (g), if a quorum of the board is not present for a properly scheduled public hearing, the hearing must be continued until the board's next regular meeting without further advertisement.

> **Comment:** Paragraph (e) essentially restates provisions in G.S. 153A-52 on continuing hearings.

(f) Conduct of Public Hearings. At the time appointed for the hearing, the chair shall call the hearing to order and proceed to allow public input in accordance with any rules adopted by the board for the hearing. Unless the board votes to extend the hearing, when the time allotted for the hearing expires, or when no one wishes to speak who has not done so, the chair shall declare the hearing closed, and the board shall resume the regular order of business.

(g) Public Hearings by Less Than a Majority of Board Members. Nothing in this rule prevents the board from appointing a member or members to hold a public hearing on the board's behalf, except when state law requires that the board itself conduct the hearing.

> **Comment:** By providing that a public hearing is deferred until the board's next regular meeting if a quorum is not present at the scheduled time, G.S. 153A-52 might appear to imply that a quorum is necessary for any public hearing scheduled by the board. Rightly understood, however, the statute concerns public hearings mandated by law, as well as discretionary public hearings that the board decides to conduct as a body. There is no legal reason why the board may not appoint one or more members short of a quorum to conduct a public hearing that is not required by law, and sometimes good reason exists for doing so. Suppose, for example, that the board wants public input on a controversial proposal to restrict door-to-door solicitation. Inasmuch as no statute directs the board to hold a public hearing prior to adopting such an ordinance, the board could choose to have individual members conduct hearings throughout the county in order to capture a broader sample of public opinion.
>
> When the board authorizes more than one member to conduct a public hearing not required by law, the safe course of action with regard to the open meetings law is to assume that the members tasked with holding the hearing constitute a committee of the board and that the hearing is therefore subject to the law's public notice and related requirements for special meetings.

Rule 37. Public Comment Periods

(a) Frequency of Public Comment Periods. The board must provide at least one opportunity for public comment each month at a regular meeting.

(b) Rules for Public Comment Periods. The board may adopt reasonable rules for public comment periods that, among other things,

- fix the maximum time allotted to each speaker,
- provide for the designation of spokespersons for groups supporting or opposing the same positions,
- provide for the selection of delegates from groups supporting or opposing the same positions when the number of persons wishing to attend the public comment period exceeds the capacity of the meeting room (so long as arrangements are made for those excluded from the meeting room to listen to the public comment period), and
- provide for the maintenance of order and decorum in the conduct of the public comment period.

(c) Content-Based Restrictions Generally Prohibited. The board may not restrict speakers based on subject matter, as long as their comments pertain to subjects within the board's real or apparent jurisdiction.

> **Comment:** Paragraphs (a) and (b) largely paraphrase G.S. 153A-52.1. In keeping with the spirit of the open meetings law, paragraph (b) likewise requires that all group members desiring to be present for the public comment period be given the opportunity to listen to the proceedings—outside the meeting room if necessary—if the room is too small to accommodate them.
>
> Paragraph (c) recognizes that the free speech guarantee in the First Amendment to the United States Constitution applies to public comment periods. In First Amendment jargon, the public comment period constitutes a "limited public forum," which means that the board may enforce reasonable time, place, and manner restrictions. Restrictions premised on the content or viewpoint of a speaker's remarks will usually be deemed unconstitutional, though the board probably may insist that speakers confine their statements to matters within the board's real or apparent jurisdiction.[116]

---

116. For an overview of constitutional limitations on the authority of local governments to control statements made during public comment periods, see Frayda S. Bluestein, *Public Comment Period Policies: What's Legal?* Coates' Canons: NC Loc. Gov't L. Blog (Mar. 15, 2016), http://canons.sog.unc.edu/public-comment-period-policies-whats-legal.

Part XI. Appointments and Appointed Bodies

Rule 38. Appointments

(a) Appointments in Open Session. The board must consider and make any appointment to another body or, in the event of a vacancy on the board, to its own membership in open session.

> **Comment:** The open meetings law expressly prohibits a public body from meeting in closed session to consider or make appointments to other public bodies.[117] It also forbids a public body from meeting in closed session to consider or fill a vacancy among its own membership.[118]

(b) Nomination and Voting Procedure for Appointed Bodies. The board shall use the following procedure to appoint individuals to bodies over which it has the power of appointment. [The nominating committee shall be called upon to make its report and recommendation(s), if any.] The chair shall [then] open the floor for nominations, whereupon board members may put forward and debate nominees. When debate ends, the chair shall call the roll of the members, and each member shall cast a vote for his or her preferred nominee. The voting shall continue until a nominee receives a majority of votes cast during a single balloting.

> **Comment:** This rule recommends that the board make appointments through a nomination procedure. An alternative way of proceeding is by motion. A member moves that the board appoint an individual, and following debate, the board votes on the motion. If the motion passes, the seat is filled. If it fails, the floor is then open to a new motion. One downside to the appointment-by-motion method is that it puts members who prefer other candidates in the uncomfortable position of having to vote against the person named in the motion. The nomination procedure allows each member to vote for his or her preferred candidate without having to vote against anyone else.
>
> As implied by the optional language in brackets, it is not unusual for boards of county commissioners to use nominating committees to consider and recommend appointments. It is likewise quite common for boards to solicit applications for appointment from citizens.

---

117. G.S. 143-318.11(a)(6).
118. *Id.*

Several statutes place significant restrictions on the board's freedom to appoint members to certain bodies. For instance, G.S. 130A-35 requires the county board of health to have a licensed physician and a registered nurse among its members.

(c) Nomination and Voting Procedure to Fill a Vacancy on the Board. The procedure described in paragraph (b) shall be used to fill a vacancy on the board, except as superseded by the provisions of G.S. 153A-27 or -27.1. If the county is divided into electoral districts, the person selected to fill the vacancy must reside in the same electoral district as the member being replaced. If the member being replaced was elected as the nominee of a political party, then his or her replacement must belong to the same party.

> **Comment:** Both G.S. 153A-27 and -27.1 establish procedures for filling vacancies on boards of county commissioners. The first statute applies to most counties, while the second statute covers the 42 counties listed therein. Many of the provisions in the two statutes are identical or similar, but some differ in important respects, especially with regard to the role of the county executive committee of the relevant political party when the member being replaced was elected as that party's nominee. Under G.S. 153A-27, the board must consult the county executive committee, but it is not bound by the committee's recommendation. In a county subject to G.S. 153A-27.1, however, the board has no choice but to appoint the person recommended by the county executive committee, unless the committee fails to make its recommendation within 30 days of the vacancy's occurrence.[119]

(d) Multiple Appointments. If the board is making more than one appointment to a body, each member shall have as many votes in each balloting as there are slots to be filled, and the votes of a majority of the total number of members voting shall be required for each appointment. No member may cast more than one vote for the same candidate for the same position during a single balloting.

> **Comment:** Paragraph (d) explains how the procedure set out in paragraph (b) works when more than one appointment is being made.

---

119. The two statutes also set out procedures for filling vacancies when the number of empty seats makes it impossible for the board to muster a quorum. Under either statute, the chair appoints enough members to make up a quorum, and the board fills the remaining vacancies. G.S. 153A-27; 153A-27.1(a). If the vacancies prevent the board from obtaining a quorum and the office of chair is empty, the clerk of court must fill all vacancies on the board in response to the request of any remaining board member or a petition from any five registered county voters. G.S. 153A-27; 153A-27.1(a). If the county falls under G.S. 153A-27.1, and the members who have left the board were elected as political party nominees, the chair or the clerk must abide by the timely recommendations of the relevant county executive committee(s). G.S. 153A-27.1(d).

(e) Vote by Written Ballot. The board may vote on proposed appointments by written ballot in accordance with Rule 30.

> **Comment:** Written ballots may also be used if the board employs the appointment-by-motion method.

Rule 39. Committees and Boards

(a) Establishment and Appointment. The board may establish temporary and standing committees, boards, and other bodies to help carry on the work of county government. Unless otherwise provided by law or the board, the power of appointment to such bodies lies with the board.

> **Comment:** With certain limitations, the board has broad authority to "create, change, abolish, and consolidate offices, positions, departments, boards, commissions, and agencies of the county government . . . in order to promote [the] orderly and efficient administration of county affairs."[120] The board may not abolish a board, commission, or agency that is mandated by law, however. For instance, G.S. 153A-344 requires any county that exercises its zoning authority to have a planning board, so a board of county commissioners that has adopted a zoning ordinance may not abolish its planning board unless it repeals the zoning ordinance.
>
> State law also constrains the board with regard to the size of certain bodies and the terms of their members. Pursuant to G.S. 108A-2 and 108A-4, for example, the county board of social services must consist of three or five members, each of whom is appointed for a three-year term.

(b) Open Meetings Law. The requirements of the open meetings law apply whenever a majority of an appointed body's members gather in person or simultaneously by electronic means to discuss or conduct official business.

> **Comment:** Official meetings of the county's appointed bodies, like those of the board of county commissioners, trigger the notice, access, and related requirements of the open meetings law, regardless of whether the body is labeled a committee, board, commission, or some other term.

(c) Procedural Rules. The board may prescribe the procedures by which the county's appointed bodies operate, subject to any statutory provisions applicable to particular bodies. [In the absence of rules adopted by the board, an appointed body may promulgate

---

120. G.S. 153A-76.

its own procedural rules, so long as they are in keeping with any relevant statutory provisions and generally accepted principles of parliamentary procedure.]

> **Comment:** The board has the power to determine the rules under which the county's appointed bodies will function, except when the rules are set by state law. Boards of adjustment, for instance, must operate in accordance with statutory provisions that regulate how they conduct business.[121]
>
> What if the board has neglected to adopt procedural rules for its appointed bodies? The absence of rules can increase the odds that meetings of those bodies will be marked by confusion. For this reason, the optional language in brackets authorizes the county's appointed bodies to adopt their own procedural rules if the board leaves them to their own devices.

Part XII. Miscellaneous

Rule 40. Amendment of the Rules

These rules may be amended at any regular meeting or at any properly called special meeting for which amendment of the rules is one of the meeting's stated purposes. Any amendment to these rules must be consistent with any relevant statutes and generally accepted principles of parliamentary procedure. To be adopted, a motion to amend these rules must be approved by a majority of the board's members.

> **Comment:** As remarked in the *Comment* to Rule 1, the board has broad authority to adopt procedural rules that do not conflict with state law or generally accepted parliamentary principles. That same authority extends to the amendment of such rules.
>
> An actual majority of board's members, rather than a simple majority of votes cast, is necessary to approve proposed amendments to these rules. Without this requirement, a minority of the members might be tempted to alter these rules when other members are absent to allow for some action disfavored by most of their colleagues.[122]

---

121. *See, e.g.*, David W. Owens, Land Use Law in North Carolina 143–58 (2nd ed. 2011) (describing the procedures that a board of adjustment must follow when conducting quasi-judicial proceedings).

122. This rule assumes that, in adopting these rules, the board has not acted by ordinance. If the board has put its procedural rules into an ordinance, G.S. 153A-45 prevents the board from adopting an amendment to those rules on the date of introduction, unless all members of the board vote in favor of the amendment.

Rule 40 should not be confused with a motion to suspend the rules under Rule 32 (Motion 6).

Rule 41. Reference to *Robert's Rules of Order Newly Revised*

The board shall refer to *Robert's Rules of Order Newly Revised* for guidance when confronted with a procedural issue not covered by these rules or state law. Having consulted *Robert's*, the chair shall make a ruling on the issue subject to appeal to the board under Rule 32 (Motion 1).

> **Comment:** Because *Robert's* was written chiefly with large assemblies in mind, many of its provisions may not be ideal for a small board. Except insofar as they embody general principles of parliamentary procedure, those provisions should be viewed as purely advisory in nature. They do not bind the board.

Appendix A. Order of Precedence for Procedural Motions

Motion	Vote Required*	Notes
To appeal a procedural ruling of the presiding officer	Majority	This motion is in order immediately after the ruling being appealed and at no other time. The member making the motion need not be recognized, and, if timely, the motion may not be ruled out of order.
To adjourn	Majority	None
To recess to a time and place certain	Majority	This motion must state the time (including the date, if the meeting will reconvene on a different day) and place at which the meeting will resume.
To take a brief recess	Majority	The presiding officer may call a brief recess at any time on his or her own authority.
To follow the agenda	Majority	This motion must be made when an item of business that deviates from the agenda is proposed or it is out of order as to that item.
To suspend the rules	Majority equal to at least a quorum	The board may not suspend provisions that incorporate state law.
To divide a complex motion	Majority	None
To defer consideration	Majority	This motion is a hybrid of the traditional motion to postpone indefinitely and the motion to lay on the table. A substantive motion that is deferred expires [100] days after the deferral date unless a timely motion to revive consideration (Motion 13) is adopted. While a deferred motion remains pending, a new motion with the same effect may not be introduced unless the board first votes to suspend its rules (Motion 6).

(continued)

Motion	Vote Required*	Notes
To end debate ("call the previous question")	Majority	Any substantive or procedural motion is potentially subject to a motion to end debate. A motion to end debate on a pending motion is not in order until every member has had a chance to speak once.
To postpone to a certain time	Majority	This motion may be used to delay consideration of a substantive motion until a designated day, meeting, or hour. While a postponed motion remains pending, a new motion with the same effect may not be introduced unless the board first votes to suspend its rules (Motion 6).
To refer a motion to a committee	Majority	If the committee fails to report on the motion within [60] days, the board must take up the referred motion again at the request of the member who introduced it. During the referral period, a substantive motion with the same effect may not be introduced unless the board first votes to suspend its rules (Motion 6).
To amend	Majority	Any substantive or any procedural motion other than a motion to appeal (Motion 1) may be amended. A motion to amend must concern the same subject matter as the motion that it seeks to alter. No more than one motion to amend and one motion to amend the amendment may be pending at the same time. Any amendment to a proposed ordinance must be reduced to writing before the vote on the amendment.
To revive consideration	Majority	This motion is in order within [100] days of the vote to defer consideration (Motion 8).
To reconsider	Majority	To be in order, this motion must be made by a member of the prevailing side at the same meeting during which the original vote was taken. The motion may not interrupt deliberation on a pending matter.
To rescind	Majority	This motion is not in order if rescission is forbidden by law.
To prevent reintroduction	Majority equal to at least a quorum	This motion is in order immediately following the defeat of a substantive motion and at no other time. If adopted, it bars the reintroduction of the failed substantive motion for [six] months or until the board's next organizational meeting in an even-numbered year, whichever comes first. If the board wishes to take up the substantive motion during the period in which reintroduction is forbidden, it must first vote to suspend its rules (Motion 6).

Note: This chart is a modified version of one originally created by A. Fleming Bell, II. Under these rules, all procedural motions are debatable, and none requires a second.

*Except as otherwise noted, the term "majority" means more than half of votes cast, a quorum being present.

Appendix B. N.C. Board of County Commissioners Procedures: Selected Statutes

Following are selected North Carolina General Statutes (G.S.) that impose procedural requirements on the board of county commissioners.

Topic	N.C. General Statute(s)
Organization, regular, special, and emergency meetings	G.S. 153A-39, -40, -443; G.S. 143-318.12, -318.13
Open meetings requirements	G.S. Chapter 143, Article 33C
Meeting location/Meeting notice	G.S. 153A-40; G.S. 143-318.12, -318.13
Meeting disruptions	G.S. 143-318.17
Rules of procedure	G.S. 153A-41
Role of the chairman	G.S. 153A-39, -40
Quorum	G.S. 153A-43
Voting	G.S. 153A-39, -44; G.S. 143-318.13
Adopting ordinances	G.S. 153A-45, -46, -47
Minutes	G.S. 153A-42; G.S. 143-318.10(e)
Ordinance book and code	G.S. 153A-48, -49, -50
Public hearings	G.S. 153A-52
Public comment periods	G.S. 153A-52.1
Board structure	G.S. 153A-34, G.S. 153A-58 through -64
Board vacancies	G.S. 153A-27, -27.1
Ethics (codes, training)	G.S. 153A-53; G.S. 160A-86, -87

Note: The above chart was prepared by Norma R. Houston, a faculty member at the School of Government.